**James Withey** is the author of the bestselling book *How to Tell Depression to Piss Off: 40 Ways to Get Your Life Back*, and is the co-editor of *The Recovery Letters: Addressed to People Experiencing Depression* and *What I Do to Get Through: How to Run, Swim, Cycle, Sew, or Sing Your Way Through Depression*. He is the founder of The Recovery Letters project which publishes online letters from people recovering from depression. James trained as a person-centred counsellor and worked in addiction, homelessness and mental health services. He lives with depression and anxiety and writes and speaks about mental health. He lives in Hove in the UK with his husband and emotionally damaged cat.

Praise for *How to Tell Anxiety to Sod Off*:

'There are two notable elements to this book. Firstly, the entertaining and self-deprecating (and funny) personal style of writing means that it is **easy to connect** with the author, and not see him as a preachy guru from on high. Secondly, the book is **packed with solid advice** for how we can relate to our anxiety in way that still allows us to live our best life. **Highly recommended**'

Nic Hooper, senior lecturer in psychology and author of *The Unbreakable Student*

'James takes a super-serious message and delivers it with a twinkle in his eye. **You end up accidentally learning loads** of stuff'

Andy Cope, bestselling author of *The Art of Being Brilliant*

'James has written a wonderfully **light-hearted, down-to-earth and practical** book that has the potential to help many people and in many ways. *How to Tell Anxiety to Sod Off* is **a joy to read**, and James' jargon-free and authentic style will appeal to all those who need help with anxiety'

Richard Nicholls, writer and psychotherapist

'A **humorous, accessible and genuinely helpful** pick 'n' mix of anecdotes and tips to help put anxiety back in its box'

Lucy Nichol, author and mental health campaigner

'As a person with anxiety who loves swearing, **this book is sodding helpful**'

Julie Cohen, bestselling author

# How to Tell Anxiety to Sod Off

## 40 Ways to Get Your Life Back

James Withey

ROBINSON

ROBINSON

First published in Great Britain in 2022 by Robinson

1 3 5 7 9 10 8 6 4 2

**Important note**
This book is not intended as a substitute for medical advice or treatment.
Any person with a condition requiring medical attention should consult
a qualified medical practitioner or suitable therapist.

A CIP catalogue record for this book
is available from the British Library.

ISBN: 978-1-47214-638-0

Typeset in Sentinel by Initial Typesetting Services, Edinburgh
Printed and bound in Great Britain by Clays Ltd, Elcograf S.p.A.

Papers used by Robinson are from well-managed forests and other responsible sources.

Robinson
An imprint of
Little, Brown Book Group
Carmelite House
50 Victoria Embankment
London EC4Y 0DZ

An Hachette UK Company
www.hachette.co.uk

www.littlebrown.co.uk

How To Books are published by Robinson, an imprint of
Little, Brown Book Group. We welcome proposals from
authors who have first-hand experience of their subjects.
Please set out the aims of your book, its target market
and its suggested contents in an email to
howto@littlebrown.co.uk

For all the Liverpool lot

# Contents

'Whoever has learned to be anxious in the right way has learned the ultimate'

Søren Kierkegaard

*I like this quote for two reasons:*
*1, it's totally true – you're going to be awesome – and*
*2, my cat is called Kierkegaard (and he's very*
*anxious, but also awesome).*

9

# Introduction

Anxiety is a pillock. Truly it is.

It's sheer, bloody terror. It feels like you've been hung upside down over a cliff, the rope you're tied to is slowly fraying into oblivion, a big countdown clock is ticking and getting louder with each click, you've been injected with seventy-five shots of organic Guatemalan espresso, someone is playing the theme tune to *Jaws* on a church organ nearby and there are crowds of people gathered around screaming, 'You deserve this, you hopeless bum wart, so *neh, neh, neh.*'

If you weren't feeling anxious before, you probably are now; I know I am, so your first instruction is to get a cup of tea and a slice of something lovely. Anything gooey will do – I'll have some carrot cake please. Find a comfy chair. If it's winter, get a blanket; if it's summer, get a fan. Get comfy, settle in.

Anxiety has been with me all my life – a hideous, terrifying companion that I couldn't shake off. It's accompanied by depression – great, eh? Who needs strawberries and cream when you can have anxiety and depression? It's been with me since primary school, followed me to secondary school, university, into my first job, into relationships, came with me abroad, to picnics by the river, to weddings, baby-naming ceremonies and stuck with me on beautiful, relaxing, sunny summer days in the park picnicking with friends (where it definitely wasn't invited).

Anxiety is rude – and mine comes in different forms at different times. Panic attacks, obsessions, social anxiety, body dysmorphia, generalised anxiety disorder, health anxiety and phobias. Get me to the anxiety Olympics and I'd win gold every time . . . but I expect you'd be on that podium standing right next to me.

We're all different, so we get anxious about different things. My husband panics when I dig up the weeds in the garden because he's become attached to them, so I have to tell him they've gone to live on a farm in the country. My cat panics at the noise from the recycling lorry; the rubbish lorry he's fine with, for some reason. Don't judge what your anxieties are about – it's pointless comparing them to others – there's no 'league of anxiety pain'. Just because you're anxious about mallard ducks doesn't mean it's any less horrendous than someone worrying about their family becoming ill.

There is no one way to help manage your anxiety, and anyone who says differently is probably selling magic beans. That's why this book has forty different ways for you to try. Feel free to alter them to suit yourself. The ways are born out of half a century of me living with it and many years as a counsellor supporting people who were also managing it. I still grapple with my terrifying companion – he's called Derek, by the way – but I've found ways of punching him in the face, laughing at him and getting on with my life despite his presence.

This book is a companion to *How to Tell Depression to Piss Off*, which you may have read ... but if you haven't, why not? Honestly, let's not get off to a bad start. It has the same format and some of the themes overlap a little, but depression and anxiety are different beasts, even if they often chum around together.

You don't need to try all forty ways in this book. I mean you can if you want, but I expect that's making you anxious, so choose the ones you want to try, give them a good go, and if they don't fit, try another. Try one, try a combination. I use different ones for different types of anxiety and depending on how I'm feeling at the time. Also, you don't need to read this book from start to finish like a traditional book; you can dip in and out – hey, start from the back if you want, or read it upside down. I mean, when *you're* upside down, not the book – an upside-down book is hard to read (and let's not make things more difficult than they already are).

I also give you permission to write all over this book. Circle things in red pen, underline sentences that particularly ring true for you. You can bend the corners of the pages that help you or draw pictures of unicorns if that works. It's not a workbook, because I hate workbooks – anxiety is bad enough without feeling you have to do loads of homework as well.

Reading about anxiety can sometimes trigger your anxiety (infuriating, isn't it?), so look after yourself. By that I mean call someone, contact a helpline, text a mate or eat some mango and raspberry ice cream if you need to. I've made the book light-hearted for that very reason.

I reckon you shouldn't need a dictionary minimised on your laptop to understand how to manage your anxiety, so this book is jargon-free and hopefully it will get you laughing a little as we go (God knows you really need some giggling when you have anxiety).

Don't underestimate the power of anxiety; nor should you ever (ever) underestimate your ability to manage it. You just need the right techniques, and a loud gobby, shouty voice.

Keep going, keep fighting, keep living – and join me in telling anxiety to sod off.

James

# 1. Pick your anxiety battles

I don't do dinner parties because I kill people.

OK, that's not entirely true; I'm not writing this from solitary confinement in HMP Strangeways. I'm an *imaginary* serial killer or, yes, if you want, let's go for a bad pun: I'm an imaginary *cereal* killer.

Sometimes I have people over for food – cold food, only ever cold food. Processed packaged cheese, pre-washed salad bags and southern Mediterranean dips have basically saved my social life. Occasionally, I might heat something up, if I've cooked it at least twenty-five times in the past, and Patrick, my husband, takes full responsibility for any deaths that may occur from underheated falafel. Soup is sometimes acceptable, but only if it doesn't have any meat in it (because I will obviously give people E. coli), otherwise I will be fretting for days afterwards that the sell-by date was wrong, that I didn't heat it up to the correct temperature or that I inadvertently put five pints of 'Ocean Spray' toilet cleaner from the bathroom cupboard into the saucepan.

The plus side to not having dinner parties is that I don't run around the kitchen shouting, 'Spatula! Spatula! Where is the bloody spatula?' Neither do I have to put up with dinner-party conversations with people called Taffy or Biffy who want to tell me about their utter nightmares of finding decent domestic help in the local area, and wasn't it all so much easier when the upper classes could live like they do on *Downton Abbey*.

I don't have to tell the difference between 'tsp' and 'tbsp' or convert American recipes from cups and spoons to . . . well, whatever you convert them to. I don't have to apologise for my unrisen soufflés (not a euphemism) while a determined bead of sweat drips off my forehead, over my nose, through my beard and into the chocolate custard. Do you have chocolate custard with soufflés? How do you make chocolate custard? Does chocolate custard even exist? See, I've no idea, and this is an excellent thing.

Can I live with not fretting over whether I've killed off my best friend with a partially baked woodcock? I certainly can. Let them eat Slovakian camembert and taramasalata. It's far better for me to have had guests over and not feel the need to take Valium, three hundred pints of Rescue Remedy and submerge myself in a bath infused with Provençal lavender.

I can function better without being the big, big boss at work and be responsible for everyone and everything.

Who needs that kind of stress? I take on extra jobs at work that interest me, that I enjoy and make my work life more meaningful.

**You see, you have to pick your battles with anxiety.**

Some anxieties I want to tackle because they get in the way of my normal life too much, or because tackling them will significantly improve my life.

I keep challenging myself around my body-image anxieties. I keep questioning, I keep trying different techniques, I keep at it because feeling good about not having a 'perfect' body (whatever the hell that is) is a sensible, healthy thing to do. I want to try to be less anxious under the hellish lighting of the TK Maxx changing rooms when I'm trying on a jumper that makes me look like an amateur sausage-maker's first attempt.

I'm working on becoming less worried about people I love dying – I know, starting small, eh? As much as I don't want to accept that we all die, being in denial about that ain't going to stop the most certain thing in all of our lives. As much as I think I have superpowers, I can't stop people dying. My anxiety will not stop this happening, but I can try to become more accepting of it and therefore less anxious. Shouting 'Just stop bloody worrying about it' at myself is not going to work.

It's going to be different for you. You might be thinking,

17

*He's worried about killing people with food? How weird is he?* You might be thinking this while simultaneously whipping up a *fricassée* de poulet *à* l'ancienne. If you are, stop for a second and for goodness' sake concentrate and make sure that chicken is cooked through.

You see, it's all about balance and challenge. Think about what limitations you can accept and what changes you want to make, and then try to make them a step at a time.

You can tackle big issues, but just in small steps. Small, reasonable chunks, one at a time. You don't eat the whole pineapple at once, unless you're a mountain tapir, so a chunk at a time – and you'll avoid heartburn too.

# 2. Go on – have a sodding tantrum

If anxiety was a person, it'd be somewhere between a doom-laden member of a Greek chorus and a petulant, over-emotional adolescent; I should know because I was one (an adolescent, that is, not a member of a Greek chorus).

You have to work against what your anxiety is saying to you because it's deliberately being overly dramatic and attention seeking.

When I tackle my anxiety, I turn myself into a contrary little git. This takes a little effort (not the git part), courage and practice, but it's totally worth it as you get to be stroppy and childlike, which is always pleasing. You have to play Anxiety Top Trumps, and the toddler card always beats the anxiety card by a thousand points.

There are hundreds of books by eminent anxiety experts telling you about the dangers of responding to situations with your inner child, but that's exactly what we're going to do here. Feels a bit rebellious, doesn't it?

Those same experts (most of whom have never had severe anxiety) also talk about being careful not to respond with anger, but again, we're going to be little tearaways and get really, really cross.

Anger is absolutely fine to use as a tool if it helps you manage your anxiety. If anyone tells you otherwise, I will unleash my full fury on their mortal souls. In a nice, peaceful, loving way, obviously.

When I began to practise this, I started with my smaller anxieties first. Before I go to bed, I always worry that the toilet light switch will somehow electrocute my husband, so I have to switch it on and off a few times to make sure (it doesn't matter if it electrocutes *me*, apparently). Neither does the evidence of it *not* electrocuting me mean that I have to stop checking it. Anxiety tells me to check the switch at least seven thousand times (OK, maybe six). It's a real pain in the arse and a complete waste of electricity.

I've gradually reduced the amount of checking. I've gone down from six times to five, to four. I've done this by talking back to anxiety and having a toddler meltdown at the same time. I say:

**'No, no no, anxiety, you ain't gonna rule me today. I WILL NOT bow down to your nonsense, I WILL NOT, NOT, NOT!'**

In my head, and sometimes in reality, I thump my fists on the floor and scream very loudly.

It also works for my larger anxieties too, although it takes a bit of practice. I routinely worry that I am seriously ill which stops me living in the moment, and instead I fixate on the idea that I'm about to die. Frankly, it would be much nicer if I worried about the idea of receiving a lifetime supply of my favourite peach and passionfruit yoghurt in the post, but anxiety has a whole other agenda. I use the same talkback approach but ramp up the tantrum level to one hundred.

**'Sod the sod off, you useless piece of antelope guttage. I will not – NOT – be a slave to your pointless pithery, your ridiculous regime of reductiveness. SOD OFF!'**

I can't claim that the words used here are in the *Oxford English Dictionary*, but it really doesn't matter. Have fun making up your own swear words – when else do you get the chance to do this?

Muster up all the bile and venom you have. Fight back; make sure your talkback and your actions are contrary to what anxiety is telling you to do, because if you don't anxiety will do all it can to take you over, like a late-running bullet train. So, stamp your feet, shout, get on the floor, pound your fists and stick out your tongue and scream:

**SOD OFF!**

# 3. Remember when your anxiety was wrong?

23

There was a time when I convinced myself I'd locked someone in a toilet.

I could see them sitting on the loo seat, weeping with despair, piles of toilet roll around their ankles, knuckles raw from banging on the door and clumps of hair torn from their head in existential agony.

Or, of course, what was more probable (to me at least) is that they were dead. With no mobile phone, they had taken to writing their final messages in lemon-scented bleach on the wall, and then collapsed from starvation and hopelessness. 'James,' they had written, 'James is responsible for my death, the careless inconsiderate bumhole, and he shall be haunted with guilt forever more, ever more, ever more, more, more . . .'

Fast forward to 3 a.m. and after a sleepless night I was pacing around my flat, wearing out the already worn carpets (from previous anxious pacing). My husband and

I were due to go on holiday that morning – how could I happily sip mojitos and appraise Cubist art in Spanish galleries if I thought I'd killed someone in the ladies' loo? You've had that problem too, right? We all have.

How could I have been so stupid as to not check the toilets before locking up the office? I hadn't seen this person leave the building so in my befuddled, stupid, anxious head the best-case scenario was that they were trapped overnight. That was me trying to do the positive thinking my therapist had taught me (by the way – 98 per cent of me was convinced they were dead).

I could see myself on holiday, sipping lukewarm macchiatos on the sun-kissed beaches of Torrevieja, served by someone whose English was vastly superior to mine (despite it being their third language), and suddenly the police would come and grab me from behind and bundle me off to a urine-soaked prison cell following orders for my European arrest warrant.

Our flight was due to take off at 9 a.m. so the completely obvious thing to do was to leave the flat at five, get the first train into work and check the toilets for a dead body.

On the train I was paranoid that other people could see my guilt and were secretly informing the police. When I got to the office the lift seemed to take three times longer than normal. My head and heart pounding, I turned off the office alarm, took a deep breath and headed for the toilets, putting a tissue over my nose to stop the smell of rotting flesh, an action I could have only seen in cheap detective dramas. I opened the door and the smell was putrid, simply awful, utterly hideous – thank goodness for the tissue.

But there was no dead body. There was nobody there at all, no one trapped, no one dead, just nobody at all; however, the cleaner had used apricot-scented bleach rather than the lemon.

What joy! I hadn't accidently killed anyone in the toilet. Oh hooray! I was free to go on holiday, suddenly I loved life, I wasn't going to prison! Oh happy days! I danced around the office which, naturally, is when my boss came in and I had to pretend I had forgotten some essential paperwork and had just stubbed my toe on a potted palm.

This is just one of the many incidences where my anxiety was completely wrong. Not just leading me up the garden path, but taking me down smelly rat-infested alleyways. It was an utter waste of time and energy; useless emotions achieving nothing at all. This is how crap anxiety is; it robs you of the present and fast forwards you into a dark dystopian future.

Anxiety had forced me to doubt myself, to ask the dreaded 'What if?' questions I know the answer to, but under its evil spell I still felt compelled to repeat endlessly: What if I'd locked someone in the toilet? What if they couldn't get out? What if they died in the toilet? What if I went to prison?

The trick is to remember **ALL** the times that anxiety has been wrong in the past. It was wrong about *The Body in the Toilet* (a lesser-known Agatha Christie novel), and I have a huge list of all the other times it's been wrong in the past too. This includes being convinced I gave a woman in a supermarket a heart attack because I reached past her for some chunky vegetable soup and gave her a shock – which led to me surreptitiously following her around the canned goods aisle to make sure she didn't collapse. I fretted for days about going to a ridiculously trendy and sophisticated birthday party of someone I didn't know. Another time I was convinced I was going to be sacked for accidently signing off an e-mail to someone incredibly important and influential, with 'lots of love' rather than 'kind regards' – there may have been three kisses too. OK, there were four. And a hug.

When we see how our anxiety has been wrong in the past, it can help our present anxiety. Anxiety repeats and plays on our particular worries; so it's likely that things you were anxious about in the past, you're anxious about now too.

When anxiety comes to me now, I look at my list (it's on my phone), and remember the same symptoms and feelings – racing heart, doom-ridden thoughts, guilt, sweating profusely, dry mouth – and I remind myself just how wrong anxiety was then. So it will be now, too. It helps me to stay in the present and tackle the feelings and thoughts more clearly.

If all else fails, I thank the gods that they stopped selling apricot-scented bleach.

# 4. You're not Nostradamus

Forgive me for being presumptuous, but I don't think you're an internationally acclaimed fortune teller who works for the United Nations, NASA and the CIA. You're not able to time travel via a portal in your bathroom sink and see what will happen in the future. Also, I have doubts you're a prophet. You're not Nostradamus or John the Baptist, or Jonah (of the whale fame). I mean, unless, you actually *are* one of those people. How spooky would that be? But my basic hunch is you're probably not.

Just because I worry about whether my cat is going to get run over doesn't mean it's going to happen. Because I'm anxious about losing my job doesn't mean it's going to come true. Because I fret about running people over when I drive a car doesn't mean it will occur. I have many, many superpowers (obviously), but I can't prophesise, I can't make those prophesies come true and I can't see into the future.

Anxiety makes you believe you might be a fortune teller, but an anxious thought is just that: a thought.

Thoughts are not facts; they're not a glimpse into what might happen in the future. Sure, there's a possibility of anything happening, but you've got to play the odds and stay in the present. If I constantly worry about losing my job it stops me from enjoying it now; there will be plenty of time to worry if I do lose it.

Anxiety is all like, 'Future, future, future, blah, blah, blah'. Basically, anxiety is useless. Think about it for a minute – how useful has anxiety ever been to you? No, I mean *actually* think about. I'll be here when you get back. I'll put sixty seconds on the clock.

How did you get on? What d'ya reckon?

I don't mean your fear instinct by the way. That can be really useful, but it's a slightly different thing. I once had to run away from a group of geese on a farm who wanted to eat me – my fear instinct was quite handy then. What I mean is your run-of-the-mill worrying about things you have no control over.

My worrying about people dying doesn't stop people dying. My anxiety about being sacked doesn't stop me being sacked. My constant ruminating, since I was sixteen, about losing my hair didn't stop those darn follicles packing their bags and moving abroad.

Your actions are what change things; worrying doesn't. Now, I'm not being flippant; I know all too well how hard this is. It's really, really hard (and I've spent far too many days not being able to go outside or fretting about having killed seagulls – see Chapter 6).

My point here is that the actual worrying doesn't achieve anything apart from dragging you down and making you more anxious. By seeing anxiety as useless and not an accurate prediction of the future, it weakens it. Anxiety needs our worrying to keep feeding it, so when we see it as weak it doesn't get the energy it needs to rule us.

Anxiety is as useless as a submarine with a fear of water, a hedge trimmer on Saturn, a macramé nappy, lingerie on a badger, etc., etc. You can spend some fun time making up your own sayings, which might help to distract from your anxiety too.

**Remember: anxiety is a false prophet.**

# 5. Name and shame

When we shame something, it reduces its power.

With anxiety we feel helpless, useless and are convinced other people are coping much better than us. But rather than feeling ashamed of our anxiety, we should turn the tables, shine a light on it, name it and shame it.

Me on the phone to a stupid man from a delivery company about a parcel.

ME: It says here delivery will be between 6 a.m. and midnight.

STUPID MAN: Yes.

ME: Well, I was just, well, I was wondering if you could maybe give a more specific time? Pin it down a bit more, you know.

STUPID MAN: No.

ME: No?

STUPID MAN: No.

ME: No?

STUPID MAN: No.

ME: Really no?

STUPID MAN: No.

ME: Oh. Right. Not even, morning, afternoon or evening?

STUPID MAN: No.

ME: Why?

STUPID MAN: The driver has to make sixty-four stops in your allotted time period within a radius of 18.8 miles. There are a number of factors that could delay them: traffic, fog, vehicular breakdown, gaining access to the property, major terrorist incidents on the A27, earthquakes, tsunami, volcanic eruption in Iceland, kidnapping of minor members of the royal family and outbreak of World War III.

ME: What about Canadian geese dancing on the motorway?

STUPID MAN: It's *Canada* geese and that scenario is also *possible* and so therefore it's *impossible* to give you a clearer time period.

ME: Not even eight to eight?

STUPID MAN: No.

ME: Nine to nine?

STUPID MAN: I see where you're going here.

ME: Oh, you do?

STUPID MAN: And the answer is no.

ME: Right. Excellent.

Anxiety is a slippery bugger, as slippery as this stupid man.

Anxiety will hide, blame us and sneak into our minds where it pretends to be us. When we feel the flutter of worry, our breathing starting to quicken, our body temperature rising, we need to shout:

## THIS IS ANXIETY!

Now, the most effective thing to do is to shout it out loud – really, really loud. However, I can see if you're in the middle of getting your feet hair waxed, waiting at the school gates in a hailstorm or in the supermarket shopping for vegan ham slices, it may not be the best time to do it, so in that case you shout it in your head instead.

The trick is to catch it when it comes; don't delay, don't wait until you get home. If your face goes slightly purple and morphs into a tightly clenched impersonation of a cat's bottom, then you can just claim it's trapped wind.

The other thing I want you to do (I'm sorry to be so

demanding) is to imagine you have a huge, industrial-sized torch. While you're shouting, shine the torch in the face of anxiety.

Just as when we stand up to bullies in the playground, when we call them what they are in front of the rest of the school, they don't feel so powerful any more. It's the same when we shame anxiety.

# 6. Catastrophise, catastrophise! (OMG! This is going to end *really* badly)

Catastrophising – taking our worries to the extreme, thinking the very worse outcome will happen – is a huge part of severe anxiety.

If I've lightly nudged an enormous seagull while cycling slowly on the seafront, I haven't left it grumpy but unharmed, happy to get on with its day of stealing ice creams; I've killed it. Maimed it. Murdered it. I'm an official seagull killer and will be sent down for thirty-five years without the possibility of parole, consigned to a cell with someone called Anthony 'No Toes' McGirth. In fact, I think I can hear the police coming now.

If I've made a small mistake at work, I'll come home convinced that my boss is on the phone to Human Resources planning my dismissal under Section 6.2 of my contract entitled, 'Being a total idiot'. I will end up penniless and homeless, stuck in a Victorian workhouse screaming for more gruel and repeatedly crying out 'Oh, what will become of me?!' to anyone who will listen.

If I've got a slight cough, I think I've either got consumption, tuberculosis or more likely aquagenic urticaria, which only thirty people have ever contracted in recorded medical history – but that still means I've probably got it.

Catastrophising is definitely a bad thing for anxiety because it exacerbates our panic and fear, but that doesn't stop it coming into our heads. It's understandable to think the worst will happen – that's just anxiety doing its thing. The trick is working *backwards* from it – that's the crucial part to managing catastrophising.

Let's take another look at the 'Seagull gate' example above. I'm cycling along the seafront, cursing at the wind coming from the wrong direction, and a massive seagull comes flying over me with an ice cream in its beak. About five thousand other seagulls (OK, maybe six) are chasing it, trying to wrestle the ice cream away from it. The seagull, let's call him Steven, shrieks, and decides the best plan is to land on the cycle path in front of me. I brake, swear and come to a stop as my front wheel ever so slightly nudges Steven's wing. He squawks at me a bit, gobbles up the ice cream – it looks like mint choc chip, in case you're wondering – and then flies off.

Now, most people would get cross at Steven for getting

in *their* way. They would shrug, tut and then carry on with their journey without giving it a second thought. Not me.

My eyes follow Steven as he flies off, expecting him to drop to the ground at any minute, utterly dead or at least flying in a downward spiral because of his damaged wing. He doesn't; he just scoots off into the distance towards the sea.

Here comes the catastrophising. Steven may have flown off, but once he's out of sight, I'm convinced he has dropped into the water, dead as a . . . seagull. The RSPB have been tailing me for weeks anyway, so they phone the police to report 'the wilful and callous destruction of a sea bird called Steven'. Nine police cars and the specialist firearms command screech to a halt and I'm pushed to the floor. Someone mutters, 'There will be no more seagull killing where you're going, mate' and kicks me in the ribs (where my wings would be, if I had them). I lose my job because no one likes a seagull killer. My family and friends disown me, change their names and go and live in the Faroe Islands to escape the shame. Even my cat can't look at me, and he hates seagulls. I go to jail, where I get daily beatings by a gang called 'The Seagull Lovers of Pentonville'. I die of bird flu a year to the day after killing Steven.

Righty ho, now let's work backwards.

Firstly, there is no gang in Pentonville prison called 'The Seagull Lovers of Pentonville'. Trust me, I've Googled this extensively. You don't go to prison for accidently killing a seagull. Police don't arrest you for accidently killing a seagull and the specialist firearms command don't turn their guns on a middle-aged, bald man on a bike who accidently killed a seagull. Your family and friends don't disown you and go and live in the Faroe Islands for accidently killing a seagull. You don't lose your job for accidently killing a seagull. The RSPB don't randomly follow people just in case they accidently kill a seagull and – most importantly of all –

## I DIDN'T ACCIDENTLY KILL A SEAGULL.

Hopefully, you can see how working backwards brings you back from catastrophising, reduces your anxiety and gets you back to where you need to be. If I can do it, so can you. *Toucan* play that game.

I'll get my coat.

39

# 7. What do you have control over NOW?!

Severe anxiety is one of the most frightening states we can be in. It feels like everything we know, everything we rely upon, has suddenly been stripped away. We are naked, scared, feel like we're going to die and have no control over our life. Anxiety has trapped us and is now in the driver's seat.

When anxious thoughts hit me, all I want is for the awful panic to go away, for it to just stop. My mood seems uncontrollable, my circumstances seem uncontrollable. I'm desperate to wrestle things back into place, but I can't. It's like a rat is trying to escape through my stomach.

Many years ago, I convinced myself I had set fire to the office where I was working at the time. I had spilled some water on the computer cable. Nothing had happened – there were no sparks, the computer didn't fizz and then explode – it was all fine. But it wasn't fine in my head.

I asked a colleague if he thought I had damaged the

computer, but he just said, 'Well, nothing happened, so it's all fine. What are you worried about?' I wanted to reply, 'Well, Barry, I'm worried that when I leave the computer it will send sparks out across the office, which will set the paper alight in the recycling bin, it will spread to the whole office, then the whole building, kill everyone and I will be responsible.' But I just said, 'Yes, I'm sure you're right. Thank you.'

I left work early, thinking that a walk would do me good, but I kept looking back at the building to see if there were flames coming out of it. There's only a certain number of times that you can look back at a building *not* on fire until people start staring, so I had to pretend to tie my shoelaces and then look back; or look at my phone and then look back; or pretend to be lost, look at the street names, and then look back. This also gives you terrible neck pain as you are walking forwards but arching your neck backwards. If only I was an owl, I thought, that would be the thing; owls can just turn their heads round 360 degrees. At that moment, I really wanted to be an owl, or anything other than me. I would have happily settled for sea turtle, aardvark or bar-tailed godwit.

At home, I couldn't settle. I kept checking local news for reports of a fire. I kept checking my phone to see if some-one from work had sent a text about the fire. I couldn't sit down, I couldn't sleep. It felt like I was caught up in a huge

41

wave, one of those massive ones you see off Honolulu, and I was just being tossed about like Poseidon's play thing. Damn Poseidon, damn that speary thing he carries with him, damn his beard and long hair, damn his stupidly muscly body which perpetuates male body dysmorphia and damn his ability to control the sea. Damn him, damn him, damn him.

No one else does this, I thought; I am a lone loon who is obsessed by ridiculous thoughts. Who keeps checking for non-burning buildings? Why can't I just be 'normal' and not be wrecked with guilt and anxiety for something that hasn't even happened?

In medieval times I would have been confined to a mud hut with a large 'BL' painted on the front door, for 'Big Loon'. Children would laugh at me as I went to collect more mud to build my mud conservatory and the elders would persuade the other villagers to throw ox dung at me.

Now, when my severe anxiety comes, I take control of at least one small thing in order to feel as though I have some power over my life. I counteract the anxiety by making decisions. Alternative, positive actions.

You don't need to do anything huge. It's not like you have to wrestle the lollipop lady to the ground and start ushering bewildered children across the road with a large pole. Nor do you have to start your own rival company to Microsoft, build a medium-sized space shuttle in your back garden or run for mayor of San Diego. Big decisions are not advisable, which is why, when I was particularly anxious one time, I ordered fifty-four red geranium plants from the internet. To be fair they look lovely in my garden now, but the delivery woman had to make six trips from the van while I gushed my apologies.

Some small but useful things I do include:

- Choose what socks to wear – always stripy, spotty or absurdly colourful.
- Make a smoothie, carefully and deliberately selecting the ingredients. I may add some vodka, which I have obviously very carefully and deliberately selected as well.
- Rearrange one bookshelf.
- Play a computer game on my phone, usually a tennis one where I can beat Roger Federer at Wimbledon, so at least I can say 'I may be anxious, but I just thrashed one of the greatest tennis players of all time.'
- Brush the cat. He's not always happy about this but he looks less like a bedraggled Highland cow, and I feel significantly better too.

What matters is that YOU are making the decision and that you recognise that you are making it while you do it.

For example, I grab the cat's brush and as I'm brushing I say to myself, 'I am brushing the cat, fur is coming off and he is looking better.' Or 'Take that Roger! Whack – that's an ace! I am the greatest of all time; not you, you big Swiss cheese of a man. I win. You lose, sucker.' Or something like that. As I'm doing it, I'm noting in my head the control that I have over what I'm doing.

This technique cements the feeling that you *do* have control of your life and aren't just at the mercy of anxiety. Once you have gained control over one small thing you feel more able to tackle the anxieties that are hitting you.

# 8. Accepting change (you're not King Canute)

45

In case you didn't realise it, you're not King Canute, the guy who thought he could tell the tide to turn back. Unless, of course, you've changed your name by deed poll to King Canute, in which case you are officially King Canute, but you're not the eleventh-century King Canute I'm talking about here.

Mr Canute – or Canutey as I call him – couldn't accept that the tide will change, no matter how harshly he spoke to it. Similarly, with anxiety we hate the idea of change because it means uncertainty, not being in control, and the possibility of something awful happening.

It would be great if we had all the say over what will happen in the future, but unless you have some special powers that I'm not aware of, I don't think you can. But listen: if you **do** have these powers, e-mail me – we can make millions together.

So, the bugger of it all is that we must try to be

accepting of change and know that it will happen no matter how much we stamp our feet and shout at the sea. Sometimes, I stamp my feet and shout at the sea anyway, but that's just to let out some inner fury about Marvel changing Spider-Man's costume in 1988. Why would they do that?

Now, let's be honest: accepting change is crap, I hate it too, but what ya gonna do? Well, you could get your feet wet as the tide comes in, but you'll spoil those lovely canvas pumps you've just bought and you'll never be able to return them, so my suggestion is, however begrudgingly, we accept change as a constant thing. We can stick out our tongues at it as we accept that fact, which I tend to think helps a lot.

Once we sort of accept change is going to happen – *shakes fist at sky* – then our anxiety levels lower, and our ability to cope with change increases. Now, you will never hear me talking about being 'resilient' – in my humble opinion this is the most unhelpful word we can use with anxiety because it implies that if we're not able to cope with change then we've somehow failed. *Shakes fist at sky* again. It's utter hogwash. If a relationship ends, someone we love dies or we lose our job, the natural and appropriate reaction is to feel sad, desperate and to struggle. What I'm talking about here is simply accepting that change will happen. When we do that, we're less shocked by it happening and our anxieties around change are reduced.

For example, I get anxious about whether work colleagues I like are going to leave. I think *It won't be the same without them. What if the new people aren't as nice? What if I hate them so much that we have to duel with pistols at dawn?* Worrying about this doesn't stop it happening, of course. Accepting the fact that it *will* happen at some point makes me less anxious because I know the reality of the situation, and don't spend all my energy fighting against something over which I have no control, living in a state of denial. Obviously, I could tie them to their desk to stop them going but there's some sort of law against that, I think.

# 9. Meh, well, I can do other stuff

I can't drive a car. I mean, I *can* legally drive a car; I managed to pass my test, finally, at the age of thirty-two, but my anxiety stops me from driving regularly. Also, I don't know the difference between a fan belt and an intake manifold, which I suspect is important to the whole process.

My anxiety tells me that if I start driving regularly then, in due course, I will hit someone, maim them or kill them. I will also kill seven fluffy white kittens which have escaped from their mother, and an old dog belonging to an old man who has no other company (I can see him crying in his bungalow) and is more than likely an internationally renowned wonderful human being/saint/deity whose lifetime work on achieving everlasting world peace was about to be published.

I can't climb K2 on the back of a pygmy goat, I can't recreate Claude Monet's Giverny garden out of Victoria sponge, I can't reach that high note in the Whitney Houston version of 'I Will Always Love You'. Life is intolerably cruel, isn't it?

At forty-nine I've finally given up my dream of winning a Grand Slam tennis final (to be fair, it's taken forty-eight-and-a-half years to accept this). But, you know what? There's other stuff I *can* do despite my anxiety.

I *can* pick up my pants from the floor using just my toes. I *can* speak to a room of hundreds of people without having a complete meltdown. I *can* arrange a bunch of flowers so that it doesn't look like a cow has chewed them. I *can* listen to people and empathise and generally try to be a good person.

Looking at the things you *can* do is not just a frilly, fake, irritating meme that you see on Instagram about self-love: 'Tell yourself you're wonderful every day'. Sure, it's that easy, eh? All my problems are solved.

In fact, it's simply part of regaining the balance that anxiety disrupts. Picture a set of old-fashioned scales – the ornate ones with weights on one side that you see in BBC period dramas. On one side is anxiety; you're sat on the other. Yes, I know you can't actually fit onto some vintage scales, but just work with me here. Anxiety is powerful, heavy and you're up in the air, terrified. Then we start to add the stuff that you *can* do.

Maybe anxiety stops you from going freelance, but you

*can* thrive in the job you're in. Maybe you can't meet up with a group of new people for the pub quiz night, but you *can* cherish the friendships that you have already.

Managing anxiety isn't a points-based system, thankfully, but you have to mark yourself up for the things you can do and not subtract points because there are things that you can't. If I wrote down all the things I couldn't do because of anxiety, we would need a much longer book than this, with numerous appendices. So what I do is count the other stuff, and that other stuff counts for a huge amount. I don't want to hear you berating yourself about what you can't do because of anxiety, because firstly it gets us nowhere and secondly, if you do, I will personally come round to your house and give you a four-and-a-half-hour lecture about all the things you *can* do, with Powerpoint slides and everything. You really don't want that, trust me.

# 10. You're havin' a laugh, ain't you?

51

My anxiety is ridiculous. It would be utterly hilarious if it wasn't so darn awful.

I offer someone a plate of biscuits, from a sealed packet, produced in a clean, sterile factory, adhering to current health and safety guidelines and the Food Standards Agency – and I still think I've inadvertently poisoned them.

I worry about whether the smile I gave to my colleague as we passed briefly on the stairs was misinterpreted. Maybe I was smiling too much and came across as creepy. Maybe I didn't smile enough and they thought I was being grumpy and cross with them. Then I spend the rest of the day making sure that my smiles to them are neither too effusive nor too subdued and I end up looking like a crazed toothy hyena.

How many kisses should I put at the end of a text? I worry about this all the time. At what point in a new relationship can you start doing kisses? With whom can you say 'love'? Should you write 'lots of love', 'much love', '*J'adore*'? Am I supposed to weigh up how much I love people first and then put in the appropriate regard at the end? Or just put 'regards'? God, it's complicated *and* totally ridiculous.

There are, of course, the marvellous times when I think that all my friends hate me and have just been pretending to like me for the past thirty years. This sends me into such a panic that I perform a ritual in my mind of imagining all their heads being cut off and, somehow, for some reason, that resets things. See, you thought *you* were weird. You ain't got nothing on me.

Anxiety is hideous pain, but, also, when we examine it closely, it's often completely ridiculous. When we start to see the nonsense of some of our anxiety spouts, we can start to laugh at it, point at it and, yes, I give you permission to utterly humiliate your own anxiety.

'You are most flipping stupid,' I say to anxiety.

'Oooh, get you, but the problem is *all* your friends hate you, they always have,' comes anxiety's ridiculous response.

'That's stupid – you're stupid, I tell you.'

'Well, hark at you! What you goin' to do? Imagine cutting their heads off again, are you?'

'YOU sir, are ridiculous, YOU spout nonsense. I see
through your flimflam. You make me worry about things
that are just ludicrous fiffle-faffle. I laugh out loud at
*you*, sir.'

I don't know why I sound like a nineteenth-century country squire, it's just the way it is.

Laughing helps shrink the anxiety. Laughter helps
control our emotions and puts our anxious thoughts into
context. Laughing also just helps – a lot.

53

## 11. Stop the multiplying.
Stop the multiplying.
Stop the multiplying.
Stop the multiplying.
Stop the multiplying.
Stop the multiplying.
Stop the multiplying.
Stop the multiplying.

I feel anxious. Then I feel anxious about being anxious. Then I'm anxious that my anxiety will never go. Then I feel anxious about the fact that I'm anxious about my anxiety never going. Then I try to stop feeling anxious, but can't, so feel anxious about that. I feel anxious that my anxiety is weird and worse than everyone else's anxiety, and that if they knew all the weird things I was anxious about they would keep a minimum of fifteen steps away and shout 'Weirdo, weirdo, unclean, unclean' at me in the streets.

This image makes me anxious. The fact that I'm worrying about having this image makes me anxious. What if I can't stop thinking about this image?

When I talk about feeling anxious to my friends, I worry that they think I'm a right cockwomble, and when I tell them I worry about what they think of me, and thinking I'm a cockwomble, I then worry that they think I shouldn't have used the word cockwomble and they're offended by the word cockwomble and will never speak to me again. If only I hadn't used the word cockwomble, then they would still be my friends. Now, they're going to tell all my other friends about using the word cockwomble and they will all hate me too and never speak to me again and I will have to live on the streets and pay people in fallen apples to be my friend . . . and all because I used the word cockwomble.

I think you get my point. Anxiety breeds anxiety. Ruminating breeds ruminating. If we don't stop it in its tracks, anxiety will multiply faster than the African driver ant, and they can produce four million eggs every twenty-five days. Impressive – but they have nothing on anxiety.

We have to turn ourselves into surgeons and do a procedure called 'anxietectomy'. I've made this up but it sounds quite convincing, doesn't it? We have to stop the multiplying because once we hit the ground running our anxiety goes faster than a greased pig on a water slide.

We need to deal with one anxiety at a time, not fifty of the buggers. What I do when anxiety starts multiplying is to simply shout:

## 'STOP'

I continue to shout **STOP** until the multiplying, well . . . stops. Then I get my surgical gloves on, face mask and errr . . . other things that surgeons wear . . . and perform the anxietectomy. Once we have stopped the anxiety multiplying we can place it in a sterilised container and deal with it. Sometimes you have to shout **STOP** more than once to get anxiety to stop breeding: it's a randy little git. It's like, enough already, get a room.

If anxiety is being particularly demanding and wanting sexy breeding time, I take out the ultimate tool of the surgeon performing the anxietectomy and bring in the novelty song. Yes, people, get prepared – it's time to bring out the big guns. Anxiety is going to stop breeding faster than a couple caught in the sand dunes by a wet spaniel named Henry.

ME: Why is that police officer following me? Have I done something wrong? Did I accidently commit a crime in the greengrocers?

**STOP!**

Have they got a truncheon? Do police officers still have truncheons? Are they going to taser me? What if he punches me in the back and I fall into the road and get run over by a delivery van?

**STOP!**

Right, you've asked for it . . .

*Agadoo, doo, doo, push pineapple, shake the tree,*

*Agadoo, doo, doo, push pineapple, grind coffee.*

Hmmm . . . not so clever now, are you? But what if the police officer wants to . . .

*To the left, to the right, jump up and down and to the knees,*

*Come and dance every night, sing with a hula melody.*

Yes, people, I'm asking you to use novelty pop songs to stop anxiety multiplying. It's probably not a technique you've read about before in any award-winning psychiatric journals.

The thing about using novelty songs is that they are so wonderfully ridiculous. Why are they pushing a pineapple? What's the point? If you push a pineapple, you just move the pineapple a little further along the kitchen worktop. Nothing ever happens (unless the pineapple is on the

edge of a waterfall or about to drop into a paper shredder).
See? Glorious nonsense. **Nonsense interrupts anxiety.**

You can choose any song you like, but in my experience
these criteria work the best.

- The lyrics have to make no sense at all.
- It has to be a happy song – no mournful break-up songs.
- There has to be a video with people doing silly dancing.
- There should be at least one person wearing a bow tie.

OK, the last one isn't mandatory. It's also a good idea to have a big selection of these songs in your head because it gives anxiety a shock. So, sometimes I use 'Macarena', at other times 'Gangnam Style' or 'Monster Mash'.

Now, bring on the singing.

# 12. Anxiety doesn't stop crap things happening

God, I hate it when people tell me I have to accept stuff. And the worst part of it is, they're probably right. Hate that. Hate them. Hate everything.

To date I have grudgingly accepted that my favourite mango and passion fruit yoghurt comes in a much smaller pot, all vegetarian sausages taste of diseased zebras, that my hair is not going to regrow however much I wish it, and no one will ever make a children's TV programme better than *The Flumps*.

Life is hard and crap, and crappy things happen. I hate that.

A few years ago, I went travelling in India and Sri Lanka. It was a trip I had saved up for and wanted to do since I was seven when I pored over travel books, marvelling at the majestic tea fields and incredible temples. I was worried though (surprise, surprise), mostly about being ill with food poisoning and it ruining my holiday. I had brought twenty-five bottles of melon-scented alcohol hand sanitiser, taken charcoal tablets for six months, had probiotic pill things to help my stomach, a full travel cutlery set and one of those drinking straws that filters out all the nasty bugs. But what would I do if I got ill? How would I manage in a foreign country? Who would look after me and pay for a private jet back to the UK? I spent hours, nay days, on the internet looking over advice that would prevent me from being ill.

But it was all OK. I didn't get ill.

I'm joking, of course. I did get ill.

Full-on food poisoning from a restaurant in Jodphur. My worst nightmare did happen. For a couple of days my insides decided to set up home in the toilet. Let's not dwell on the details.

I realised a few things as I was sat in bed in my hotel watching reruns of American sitcoms and sipping water.

- Sometimes crap things do happen, no matter how much we don't want them to.
- Anxiety doesn't stop the crap things happening.
- My worrying about being ill took up way more time than actually being ill.
- I will never look at naan bread in the same way.

On the third day, I rose again, carried on my way to

Varanasi and then flew to Sri Lanka. My tummy was sore, but I'd survived!

Anxiety is not some all-purpose antibiotic space shield that can destroy the possibilities of bad events happening in our lives. We can fret and worry, just like I did before I went travelling, and still bad things can happen. We're not perfect; life isn't perfect. It's just life, it's a bugger, and the quicker we come to realise that our anxious thoughts don't counteract the terrible things that happen to us, the easier it becomes to manage our anxiety and for it to lessen.

# 13. The Anxious Feelings Committee

63

I want to take you to a museum. Get your best tartan slacks on, bring a flask of coffee, some of your homemade banana bread and we'll catch the number 62 bus. Fear not, we're not going to see an exhibition of rusty nineteenth-century engineering sprockets. We're going to examine our anxious feelings and, because I'm lovely, I'll take you out for cake and cocktails afterwards.

We get to the museum and try to find our anxious feelings in the glass cases, but we can't find them. We look upstairs; we ask the museum assistant who looks at us in a strange way. The thing is we can't find our anxiety in a museum because it's not a factual thing. Sorry for the wasted trip. We'll still go out afterwards though, hey?

Our anxiety is a group of feelings but *not* a factual thing. It's a group of bloody awful sensations, but feelings aren't facts. It's worth repeating that: **feelings aren't facts**.

If we put anxiety under a microscope, it wouldn't show up; you'd just have a group of scientists scratching their heads, going 'Where the feck did it go?' My feelings are real in my head – they are authentic to me, I am experiencing them – but they're not facts that have been verified by an objective, independent committee.

If I presented my anxious feelings to the Anxious Feelings Committee about, let's say, whether a guy who looked at me strangely on the train thought I was ugly, it would go something like this.

COMMITTEE: Mr Withey, what do you think happened?

ME: We were on the train and that man looked at me and thought I was ugly.

COMMITTEE: [*To the Train Man*] Did you look at him and think he was ugly?

TRAIN MAN: No. I looked at him because I thought I knew him.

COMMITTEE: And you don't think he's ugly?

TRAIN MAN: I didn't even think about it.

ME: But he *really* stared at me.

COMMITTEE: Did you?

TRAIN MAN: Yes, because I thought it was someone I used to work with. Plus, I was looking at his hat.

ME: Ah! So, you hated my hat, *that's* what was going on.

COMMITTEE: Is that true?

TRAIN MAN: No, I was thinking that I should buy myself a similar hat.

COMMITTEE: And how can we verify what you were thinking?

TRAIN MAN: I sent a message to my friend telling her I'd seen a hat that I want for my birthday.

ME: And I bet this 'message' also said I was ugly.

COMMITTEE: Can we see the message please?

TRAIN MAN: Yes.

COMMITTEE: So, it says here, 'I have just seen the most awesomest hat on this guy on the train and I want it for my birthday'. Then some sort of emoji.

TRAIN MAN: It's a smiley face with a hat on.

COMMITTEE: Interesting. I don't think we've seen that emoji before at the committee, have we? [*Murmuring of agreement*]

ME: Can we please focus on what he was thinking about me?

COMMITTEE: I think we've established he didn't think you were ugly. Case closed.

ME: Yeah, well, y' know, OK, fine, whatevers, I think *you* are all ugly. [*Walks out in a huff*]

I was assuming my anxious feeling was a fact. I do this all the time, so now I take that anxious feeling to the Anxious Feelings Committee for verification.

Our anxieties and emotional reactions stem from so many different things: our childhood, our imagination, our fantasies, our lack of self-esteem, our experiences of bad relationships, bullying and abuse. When we react to a feeling it's often distorted and therefore can't be trusted as something true or factual.

There are facts and there are feelings. Getting the two confused makes our anxiety much, much worse, so it's important to separate them out.

# 14. It's, like, *sooooo* boring

I get really bored of my anxiety. It's so predictable.

I have to go to a party where I don't know anyone, so, of course, here comes anxiety. I have to call someone on the phone, rather than hide behind a text message – instant anxiety, naturally. I have to tackle a lobster in a restaurant (I'm not paying, obviously) with those weird claw-crushing things, an oversize napkin and a bowl of lemon water; I know that anxiety will creep up and convince me the lobster will fly across the room and hit the woman sitting by the men's toilets on the head. She will scream, the candle in front of her will set the tablecloth alight, which will set off the sprinkler system, which will flood the whole restaurant and all the waiters will be out of work, their families won't have any food and it will all be my fault.

Blah, blah, blah. BORING, BORING, BORING.

These days, the way I treat anxiety is to roll my eyes to heaven and scoff, 'Oh, I see it's you again, how *very* tiresome.' If you can do a passable imitation of Princess Margaret exhaling cigarette smoke, it helps a lot too.

If we change our reaction to anxiety, it starts to shrink. Anxiety loves it when we get upset and worried. It feeds on our nerves and panic attacks, just adores it. So, starve it with disdain.

You know that lame joke your uncle always makes at a family wedding? React to anxiety just like that. You know when a politician comes onto the news and refuses to answer any direct questions? React to anxiety just like that. You know when you meet someone at a party who only wants to talk about their oh-so-perfect life, which comprises holidaying in southern Sardinia with minor social media influencers and restoring a medieval chicken coop in Gloucestershire into their third home, and telling you how their children are so advanced they were approached by both Oxford and Cambridge universities before their eighth birthday? React to anxiety just like that (and imagine punching them a little).

Basically, you need to respond to anxiety like a blasé, disinterested French teenager being lectured by their parents for getting caught playing truant from school. I give you permission to shrug, tut, examine your nails, look anywhere else apart from where you should be looking, yawn without any attempt to conceal it and audibly breathe out with exasperated ennui. Finally, I actively encourage you to use the phrase 'Yeah, well, whatever.'

It's about disrupting anxiety's power. It's about not letting it seep into you. It's about saying to it that you're tired of its influence on you.

It's about realising that you are stronger than anxiety, because, trust me, you are.

69

# 15. Jump around

A few years ago, I thought I left a tap dripping in the bathroom sink when I went away for the weekend.

My anxieties around leaving domestic appliances on have been with me for years and have extended to worrying about the boiler self-combusting and the oven turning itself on. Anxiety really is SUCH a lovely thing, isn't it?

I had brushed my teeth before leaving for the train but had no memory of turning off the tap. In my head, this meant one of the following scenarios had occurred:

- The tap dripped normally into the sink for a few hours, then somehow blocked the sink. I don't know how, but it had. This flooded the flat, caused a fire and burned down the whole building.
- The tap dripped normally into the sink for a few hours, but I'd somehow put the plug in the sink. I don't know how, but I had. This flooded the flat, caused a fire and burned down the whole building.

- The tap dripped normally into the sink for a few hours, then somehow it had exploded. I don't know how, but it had. This flooded the flat, caused a fire and burned down the whole building.

The final scenario whirling around my head – which I was trying to ignore as much as possible– was that the cat had come into the bathroom, started drinking the water from the tap, got his tongue stuck . . . and when he eventually pulled it out, the tap broke. I don't know how, but it had. This flooded the flat, flooded the cat, caused a fire and burned down the whole building.

My friend Nick, who has a spare key, was feeding the cat so I phoned him, you know, just to check that . . . well, just to check that the cat was OK. I mean, it had been thirty minutes since I left, anything could have happened. My body was frozen with worry.

ME: Hi! Thanks so much for feeding the cat.

NICK: No problem. I'm here now, he's had his breakfast and he's fine.

ME: Excellent.

NICK: Great.

ME: Ummm . . .

NICK: Yes?

ME: No, no, it's all fine, thank you.

NICK: Have a great weekend, I'll head home now.

ME: Yes, thank you.

NICK: Is there something wrong, James?

ME: Wrong, what? No? NO. No. Definitely not. No.

NICK: There is something wrong.

ME: No, honestly, it's nothing.

NICK: I know what's wrong.

ME: Oh, you do? Oh good – I knew you'd understand.

NICK: It's all fine, you don't need to fret, I gave him the tuna-flavoured food just as you said, and I've saved the chicken for later. I didn't get them mixed up.

ME: Yes, thank you. That's *exactly* what I was worried about. Perfect. Ummm . . . I'm just wondering, ummm . . . where is the cat at the moment?

NICK: I'm not sure, he may have gone out after he ate, I think.

ME: You know what's funny? I mean, HILARIOUS – sometimes the little bugger goes into the bathroom and drinks from the tap!

NICK: OK.

ME: I know! What are cats like eh? *So* funny, dear me. I caught him once, filmed him on my phone, uploaded it onto YouTube, but it's only got three views.

NICK: That's a shame.

ME: Tragic really. Terrible. I'm just wondering if he's doing that now, you could film him, maybe?

NICK: Alright . . . I can check, I guess.

ME: Only if it's not too much trouble, don't want to put you out. Only if you really want to.

NICK: Right. So, I'm in the bathroom. He's not drinking from the tap. I'm not sure where he is.

ME: Not to worry. Is the . . . errr . . . is the tap dripping at all, would you say?

NICK: The tap?

ME: Yes.

NICK: Is it dripping?

ME: Hmmm.

NICK: No.

ME: Great, thanks, bye. [*Puts phone down*]

For goodness' sake.

Of course, the scenario that I had brushed my teeth and then turned off the tap didn't enter my head.

Rather than having Nick on speed dial all the time for any anxiety-related emergencies, I try to live with the uncertainty – and moving my body helps this massively.

Anxiety wants to keep me in one spot, dwelling,

turning over the different possibilities of how my life will end in disaster. Its aim is to make you curl up in the foetal position, slowly rocking from side to side and muttering. Anxiety wants me hiding under my duvet with the light out.

You have to do the opposite of what anxiety is telling you to do.

Physically shaking off the anxious feelings sounds a bit odd on the face of it, but I find that if you don't get moving, it will stick inside you and get worse. Anxiety has to shift, and moving the body helps this – I don't know why, it just does. Anxiety is a particularly physical illness that brings with it heart palpitations, sweating, hot flushes, dry mouth and shaking. When we move it feels like things are changing, the world is still turning and you're moving and carrying on despite anxiety.

I usually get on my bike and cycle. I like the feeling of going somewhere, the movement and sense of progression. Sometimes the anxiety is so bad I struggle to move my legs as fast as I would normally, but each turn of the pedal is important and helpful. Other times I will go the gym and pretend I'm a Norwegian cross-country skier on the cross-trainer machine thingy. I overtake everyone and win the Olympic gold medal while also beating the world record by three hours. I'm bloody awesome. It's fine to have gran-diose thoughts when you're physically trying to release anxiety because it counteracts the crap that anxiety is throwing at you, telling you you're worthless. You're not worthless; you're a frigging gold medal-winning Olympic cross-country skier for goodness' sake!

There's loads of stuff you can do physically to shake anxiety off. You can disco dance in purple hot pants, pretend to be a hyperactive meerkat behind your sofa or recreate all seven heptathlon events in your bedroom. I'm not judging – others might if they see you through the window, but I won't – so shake your bloomin' booty.

# 16. Unfriend Derek

Derek is my anxiety monster.

He's a pillock. He follows me around and every so often screams 'Surprise, you twat, you're going to die.' It pays to be able to recognise his voice and then unfriend him.

Derek calls me very insulting names. His voice is very different from mine so when he speaks, I realise it's him and take action.

This is me having a conversation with my friend Sam over dinner – see if you can spot the douchebag that is Derek.

SAM: Did you see that programme with the Argentine penguins dancing to ABBA?

ME: I did, so adorable. I don't think I should eat this chocolate brownie.

SAM: I mean, you could even see their wings flap when they played 'Dancing Queen'.

ME: They really were 'having the time of their life', weren't they? If I eat the brownie, I'll put on weight.

SAM: I know! With a bit of rock music, they were fine.

ME: Maybe if I eat half the brownie, maybe then it would be OK.

SAM: What did you say?

ME: I said, the one with the lovely eyes looked a bit like Benny.

SAM: OMG! I thought that too.

ME: I'll be fatter and more hideous and more disgusting.

SAM: I'm going to watch it again and see if I can spot Björn, Agnetha and Anni-Frid. Or should I say Anni-Fridge!

ME: Oh yes, of course, that's funny because it's cold and penguins like cold. Maybe I should ask for the brownie to be taken away and order something else, like the unsweetened frozen lemon water, but without the lemons.

SAM: Anni-Fridge! Honestly, I don't know how I do it sometimes.

ME: You really are very, very funny. But if I order something else Sam will think I'm weird. Maybe I can say I'm full up and just not eat the brownie. Or, or, I could accidently drop it? But then they might bring me another one. Bugger, bugger. BUGGER!

SAM: What?

ME: I said the burger was delicious.

SAM: Oh, it was. I was in the mood for a . . . burger and I got the chance!

ME: You fat sicko, you can't just eat the brownie, and now you look like you're staring at it in a bizarre way. Maybe Sam thinks I'm attracted to the brownie? Oh god, I need help. Who do you phone about being attracted to baked goods?

WAITER: How were your desserts?

ME: Oh, really lovely. Thank you.

SAM: It's Friday night, the lights are low, we were looking for a place to go.

WAITER: OMG, did you see that programme with the Argentine penguins dancing to ABBA?!

ME: [*Exits stage left*]

Derek is in my head and sometimes slips out into my speech.

Creating a persona for your anxiety helps because we can divorce it from ourselves, which helps us look at it more objectively and talk back to it. You can have Derek if you want, I'm *really* not precious about him, but I would spend some time thinking about how your anxiety sounds and build up a picture of it.

Once you've got your anxiety persona, you can start to change it. Derek's tone of voice started off as frightening and doom-laden, like a Russian villain from a James Bond film: 'James, bad things are going to happen to you. Be warned: your time will soon be up.' Over time I've changed him to sound whiny and pathetic instead – it gives him less power. Now he sounds like a three-year-old who can't have a fifth jam doughnut. Listen to the difference between these two sentences:

Scary, frightening voice: 'I'm going to be ill, I'm going to be sick, I can't believe I've been so stupid.'

Whiny, pathetic voice: 'I'm going to be ill, I'm going to be sick, I can't believe I've been so stupid.'

Can you see how the second one has much less impact than the first?

Just for fun, I also dress Derek up in terrible clothes. Think of it as Anxiety Barbie (which I am totally trade-marking, so get in touch, Mattel). Derek has a terrible combover, a food-stained black jacket that is three times too big for him, and lashings of dog hair on the shoulders. He's a real catch.

# 17. Wiggle your finger and watch it waggle

My anxiety often reaches such a peak that a super-fuelled terror overtakes my body.

I get physical spasms, huge body convulsions, my breathing increases, I can feel my heart pounding in my chest, my head starts to throb, I feel dizzy and my stomach lurches.

As humans we're pretty rubbish at concentrating on two things at the same time, so when this extreme anxiety occurs, I focus on one part of my body rather than my mind; it anchors me and helps disconnect from my mind playing silly buggers.

I don't do anything fancy or spiritual; in fact usually I try to concentrate on the funniest part of my body. (No not *that* – take your mind out of the gutter please. Honestly, this isn't that sort of book.)

Sometimes, I'll focus on my toes, trying to feel each one in turn, and attempt to move each one independently of the others. Or, more usually, I'll wiggle my little finger about for a while, pretending it's a harmless snake going for a walk down my high street, looking for some fruit at the market, perusing the second-hand bookshops and buying a jam doughnut at the bakery. Other times, just to mix things up a bit, I'll twitch my nose, imitating the proboscis monkey (it's worth looking these dudes up, they're truly awesome).

81

To be honest, you can choose any part of the body to focus on – making it weird just seems to help me for some reason. Connecting to your physicality when your mind is tricking you into terror makes your brain go, *Oh, your finger is wiggling, how about that?* It slows your thoughts down and distracts anxiety back to a manageable level.

Other times I'll do the complete opposite. Now, hold on a second – I know that seems to make no sense, but hear me out. Usually watching my finger wiggle does the trick, but at other times I'll deliberately concentrate and observe what's going on with my body. So, I'll say to myself, 'That's your heart racing, that's you sweating, that's you feeling dizzy.'

The important thing about this technique is to **notice, but not let it soak in**. You look at the bath, notice the steam, the smell of the bath salts – but you don't get into the bath. You're looking from a distance at what's happening to you and trying not to absorb it any further. This creates some space between the physical effects and the impact they're having on you, giving you time to go, 'Oh, of course, this is anxiety doing this to my body, I get it.' That space leaves you room to slow down your thoughts, and in turn your body symptoms start to lessen.

# 18. Big up yourself

Anxiety is a terrible, terrible thing to live with. Anxiety is
exhausting. Anxiety is truly bloody awful.

The problem is that Derek, the idiot anxiety monster
(remember that bum wipe?), convinces me I'm worthless.
He says that I should be stronger, more resilient, be able to
carry on like other people, to keep going without crying,
without worrying, without panicking. He tells me I have
anxiety because I'm a weak, pathetic, flimsy piece of litter
blowing around in a dirty, urine-infested city-centre alley.

I suspect you feel like this too.

I've spent a lot of time thinking about all this stuff and I
am here to declare that:

**We have to rethink all the negative crap we
think about ourselves for having anxiety AND
we are officially bloody incredible.**

Derek is not going to suddenly turn around and tell me

how brave I am and how much tenacity I have for living with anxiety, so I have to do it for myself. Crap, isn't it? But the thing is it pays dividends to big ourselves up. It's also the truth that we are amazing for managing this; we truly are. We are incredible for dealing with anxiety and carrying on.

What I've realised is that having criticised myself for having anxiety since I was seven years old has achieved a big fat nothing. Zilch. Nada. Not a sausage.

It hasn't reduced my anxiety, it hasn't helped me manage my anxiety; in fact, all it's done is *increase* my anxiety, so now I apply some compassion to myself which helps far more.

Also, while we're on the subject, for goodness' sake let's stop judging ourselves for having anxiety. I spend about 45 per cent of my life telling people not to judge others and the other 55 per cent telling *myself* not to judge others, and yet when it comes to judging myself and my anxiety, for some reason I think this is perfectly acceptable. What a hypocrite. And yes, I'm sorry to say this, but if you judge your own anxiety then we're in the Hypocrites' Club together. (The first rule of the Hypocrites' Club, by the way, is to try to not be a hypocrite.)

I keep a few simple phrases on my phone to remind myself to be compassionate towards myself and not judge myself. You can steal mine if you want – I'll bill you later.

- 'You're hurting, anxiety is hard and you're doing really well.'
- 'You're managing to survive this when anxiety is trying to bring you down, keep going.'
- 'You're doing the best you can, that's really good when anxiety is causing you so much pain.'

You don't need to go over the top at the start, because it will sound silly and you won't believe yourself.

85

- 'I have anxiety and I am the monarch of the whole frigging world! I am more powerful than every human being and all the sheep in that field over there.'

Also, you don't need to go to the local patisserie and declare how brave you are.

- 'Good morning. Oh, everything looks so yummy. Yes, OK, I think I'll have a custard slice; two almond croissants; a large white bloomer; thirteen, no wait, fourteen pains aux chocolats; a raspberry millefeuille; and did you know I am beautiful, I am clever, I am talented, I am caring, I am hard-working, I am skilled? And most of all I am modest.'

If you do decide to do this – and, for the record, I have no real objection to public declarations in shops selling baked goods – I want to see the YouTube video please.

Developing a compassionate and congratulatory attitude towards ourselves in turn helps how we view ourselves and bolsters our ability to manage our anxiety.

It takes a little while to get into the habit of doing this, and it takes some effort because anxiety, and society as whole, take a dim view of vulnerability and personal struggle but – and I can't stress this enough – this is absolute camel poo. Don't listen to those people who say we should hold it together, get a grip, not be a snowflake, grit our teeth, get on with it, stiff upper lip, etc. I give you permission to throw camel poo at them.

The more we practise, the easier it gets. Imagine you have a large shield, like a superhero's. You can embellish it however you like. When you hear these statements – either from you or someone else – hold up the shield and, ping! Let them bounce off.

You just need to remember that the fact that you're living and managing anxiety makes you pretty darn special in my book, and I hope in time you can tell yourself that too.

You are really incredible for managing your anxiety.

# 19. Be like my friend's dog

I'm on a walk with my friend and their dog. My anxiety is bouncing around the trees in the forest. It feels so real I can't believe other people can't see it. Sometimes, it's so bad that it stops me being able to walk properly and I stumble into the muddy puddle that I was trying to avoid.

I'm trying to keep up with the conversation; chatting about mutual friends, how awful politics is at the moment and the extortionate price of bananas. I try smiling and laughing, but it's such a huge effort. I'm certainly not convincing anyone that all is well.

My friend goes off to the toilet and it's just me and the dog. We look at each other for a while, me trying to work out what the dog is thinking; the dog only interested in when her owner is coming back, and we can set off again. I start talking to the dog, obviously.

'Are you worried too, dog? Are you anxious about work and relationships, and failing at things, embarrassment and the price of bananas?'

The dog licked her chops, sighed and went to sleep. A little disrespectful to be honest. I'm no dog behaviour expert but I don't think she cared about my questions.

Then I realised that my friend's dog doesn't care about what happens, other than what happens *now*. Dogs aren't too bothered about upcoming local elections, potential nominees for the Golden Globes or possible economic collapse in the Republic of San Marino. They would be bored by my ruminations about whether the Bank of England is going to raise interest rates in the next five years, and if cerise ruffles are going to make a comeback on the Milan catwalks this spring,

What they care about is **now**: running through the woods *now*, being happy *now*, getting treats *now* and, unfortunately, sniffing other dogs' poos *now*. If only we could all be dogs. Oh, the freedom of peeing against a lamp-post instead of faffing around with a blasted toilet. The stuff of dreams.

Anxiety is all about the future – so what might happen if we were more like my friend's dog?

Now, I'm not suggesting we can live entirely in the present all the time, as some fake-tanned fake Instagram guru may advise; this is just impossible nonsense. What I'm suggesting is that, when we can, we try to think a bit more about the here and now, because it's a useful guard against anxiety escalating.

My aim each day is to try to be an eighth of my friend's dog. I'll take the tail, but you can have any part you want – it's a decent-sized dog. I might worry about whether I'll be alone in my old age, but then I also make sure I look around and take in where I am now, today, what I'm feeling and, if I can, I'll go in search of some beauty that makes me happy.

I confess I try to *become* my friend's dog, like a dreadful exercise you had to do in drama at school. I'll try and get into her mind, that is so wonderfully preoccupied with the present, and it helps to ground me where I am for a few minutes and not launch me into the future.

Also, if in doubt, just say 'woof' out loud three times (this always makes me smile). Try it now; put the book down and say 'woof, woof, woof' out loud.

Helps, doesn't it?

89

# 20. Express yourself (Madonna does)

I'm having horrifically anxious thoughts.

My heart is pumping the blood around my body at the pace of Speedy Gonzales on cheap amphetamines. My eyes are darting around the room trying to find anything to soothe me. Sweat is starting to build up on my back and my breath is coming out like a wincing piglet.

'You just need to calm down,' says my friend, shouting at me.

'What?' I say. 'What?!'

'You're panicking – you just need to calm down.'

'Oh, you think I should just "calm down"? Excellent suggestion, I never thought of that. Sure, I will just calm down right now. See? Done – all f**king calm, my anxiety is gone like a puff of smoke from a magician's wand. I'm now ready to go to sleep like a baby bunny wrapped in cotton wool. Now I can rest on a cloud, meditating to the sound of gentle Japanese wind chimes and a cup of camomile fricking tea!'

Whenever someone says 'calm down', I know they've never experienced severe anxiety. Seriously, if someone saying 'calm down' got rid of our anxiety we would have it recorded on our phones to press play whenever we felt the slightest twinge of worry.

We do need to express our anxiety though; it has to be let out. Unfortunately, it will come out through our body and our intrusive thoughts, but it pays to take other approaches to help too.

I don't paint pet portraits, I don't knit, I don't abseil down mountains and, if I'm honest, I don't sing well – it's unbecoming because although I like to think I have the voice of a high-ranking angel, I actually have the voice of a shrieking mountain goat. So I do other stuff to express my anxiety. I write, I take photographs to record lovely things and lovely people, I cycle, I try to create a garden with some likelihood of success (i.e., choosing plants that won't die) and I like arranging stuff in my home.

When expressing your anxiety, neither the product nor how well you can do something is important; process is *everything*. So, who gives two hoots if your drawing of a vulturine guinea fowl looks like a zebra if it's helped your anxiety? Don't worry if your Jaffa cake drizzle loaf has sunk in the middle, so long as the making of it has lessened your anxious thoughts. Don't fret that your ceramic vase has ended up looking much too phallic to show to your mother-in-law, if you've let out all your anxiety while creating it.

This is why I don't get too bothered by middle-aged men in orange Lycra shorts overtaking me on the cycle lanes. It's not about who can go faster or cycle for longer; it's about me and my anxiety. It may sound selfish but it's *me, me, me*. You have to think of yourself and what helps you to let out your anxiety.

It might take a bit of time to experiment and see what works best for you. If home tattooing isn't working, try stone skipping at your local reservoir. If dressing up as your favourite superhero isn't doing it, get cracking with volcano surfing. Don't pre-judge it; don't get caught up in 'well that will never work for me' type of thinking; just give it a go. The cliché of 'what have you got to lose?' springs to mind. Blooming clichés, always being bloody true – infuriating, isn't it?

A friend of mine swears by painting by numbers to help manage their anxiety; another goes pony trekking once a month; someone else I know crochets scarves for family members – they all have *a lot* of scarves, and some may have ended up in the charity shop, but it doesn't matter; all that matters is that it helps.

Oh, and you just might want to check out one of my

other books, titled *What I Do to Get Through*, which has loads of accounts of how hobbies and activities help your mental health. That's my massive plug over. Actually, you may want to decorate your own bath and sink plugs – that could be great, couldn't it?

# 21. You get prizes for survival

I'm back home in my flat after visiting some friends and their beautiful new baby. I had a lovely cuddle with the newborn, until they started to cry and I handed them back to Dad. As I did so the baby's arm got a little stuck, but was easily sorted out by their father. These baby transfers are sometimes a little difficult, aren't they? But all was well.

Except, it wasn't well – I mean, not with me, not in my head. On my walk home I thought about how badly I handed the baby over and became convinced that, somehow, I had hurt their arm. But obviously, because this is frigging anxiety, I didn't think I had just created a little bruise; I thought I had broken the baby's arm. Then the broken arm would infect their blood, create gangrene (you can tell that I'm a renowned paediatrician, can't you?) and the baby would end up in intensive care in hospital and probably die.

Basically, the thought that I had broken or killed my friends' new baby was so appalling that my mind couldn't contain it. It was a horror so dreadful that my brain didn't know how to process it, and reality started to twist and detach. It's like an out-of-body experience where you feel the world has irrevocably changed, turned on its head and nothing will ever be the same again. You feel that your body will combust, that death is imminent. And at times, that actually feels like a blessing.

My mind starts a mutiny against me. I despair of my life. I wonder why I can't manage life 'like a normal person'. I start to question why I'd want to live with such extreme, terrifying emotions and then often suicidal thoughts occur.

I suspect you know these feelings too. Sucks, doesn't it? As I keep saying – and I'll probably repeat it at some point, I'm afraid – don't ever downplay how awful anxiety is. Don't let anyone tell you that you're not resilient enough. This is a terrible, terrible thing you're living with, and having suicidal thoughts with extreme anxiety is totally understandable. Our brain says, 'Why would I want to live in such a state of terror?', so we want to do anything to get rid of that excruciating feeling.

You'll be pleased to know the baby was fine: there was neither break nor bruise. As my friend told me when I confessed how worried I was, 'They're quite bendy things really, James.'

For surviving these episodes of severe anxiety on a

regular basis, you deserve a prize. I don't give out actual prizes, you understand – you can't have a five-foot silver gilt cup with flowing blue ribbons. However, I have invented the 'The Panics', a series of imaginary awards for when you get through these hideous feelings. You are automatically nominated, and the marvellous thing is when you survive these episodes, you win, so hooray! See, who needs an Oscar? Please feel free to make a grand acceptance speech, maybe tear up a bit and, of course, the most important thing is to ensure that you thank me profusely. Something along the lines of, 'I can't believe I've won, but I really couldn't have done this without James; I give this award to him, my mentor, my guardian, my swami, my sage, my saviour.' Anything like that will do.

When I'm in the midst of this existential shock I practise lots of other techniques covered in this book, but I also remind myself that I'm still here and surviving it. In order to do this, I keep looking at my watch, see the seconds tick by and – glorious pun alert – clock that time is passing and I'm still living.

You have to ground yourself in the present because anxiety is wanting to push you forward towards catastrophe. I sit, watch the seconds pass and repeat, 'I'm still here, I'm still here, I'm still here.'

Now, I can see that if you're saying this on the number 48 bus then you might get a few looks, but sod 'em. Keep doing it or you can just repeat it in your head if you want.

The excruciating panic and fear will peak; it *will* get better. The body isn't designed to live in a state of sheer terror for a prolonged period of time; it will send you into numbness or start to ease. You can track it by imagining you are a climber scaling the anxiety mountain, it will feel worse and worse, then peak. Then it will start to fall, a little bit at a time.

The bravery of surviving each second of what seems like the ultimate terror is a huge achievement, and evidence of your ability to carry on and survive.

## 22. Be a tree

Anxiety makes you want to run away. It's part of our primitive 'fight or flight' instinct, which was useful when we were chased by woolly mammoths and sabre-toothed whatsits. Anxiety experts are continually talking about this, but it never actually helps my anxiety to understand that I was once chased by a man-eating animal; it tends not to happen in the UK these days.

What does help me is pretending to be a tree.

OK, so I can see you sniggering at the back. Is there something you want to share with the whole class?

To be fair, when I was first asked to stand in the middle of a room in a converted barn on the Isle of Mull and imagine I was a curly willow, I had my misgivings. I'll admit it: I scoffed very loudly and refused to take part in 'such pretentious ludicrousy'. I sulked in the corner instead.

I'm never good with this kind of stuff. Whenever I'm on a training course and have to introduce myself at the start by 'telling a funny story', I cringe and squirm. Dave, the guy before me, usually makes everyone even more uncomfortable by recounting a story about a Hoover attachment. My urge to escape from the room straight through the window, despite being on the fourth floor, is unspeakably strong.

But back in the barn on Mull, I started to feel sorry for the facilitator, Indigo, with her Tibetan rainbow jumper, purple tie-dyed hareem pants and seventeen wooden arm bracelets, which jangled every time she moved.

'What you need to DO,' says Indigo, who had the strange habit of shouting certain words, 'is to IMAGINE that you are a tree, and your roots are going through the FLOOR.'

I looked at my feet and tried to imagine some roots springing from my Nike trainers. It will ruin them, I thought, these cost a fortune and I'm sorry, I am not about to make holes in them just to satisfy Indigo and her tree fetish. If she wants to obsess about trees, well, she can do that in the privacy of her own home with a cup of herbal tea, some anti-bacterial gel and a horticultural catalogue. If she wants, she can invent a new dating app for her and other tree delusion-oids called 'Timber'.

'It's a great way to manage stress, PANIC and anxious thoughts. You are STRONG, you can't be MOVED not matter how strong the wings of anxiety ARE. Feel those roots, FEEL them I tell you!'

I swear I'd seen an all-male vocal harmony group called 'Wings of Anxiety' playing in my local pub last month.

'FEEL the roots entering Mother Earth, FEEL the soil give way and FEEL how anchored you are.'

The bizarre thing was, I started to feel sturdier. I could sort of feel the roots going into the earth. What is this wizardry, I thought – what dark forces are at work? Is Indigo a freelance shaman who just happens to come from Kirkcaldy? Why am I suddenly feeling more upright and not so stressed? Resist, I told myself, resist the forces of evil that have taken hold of you! Counteract the spell by pretending to be a flower. Is that the opposite of a tree?

After standing there for a while, I realised that Indigo was not a shaman, an alien, or a purple witch; she was just a woman from Kirkcaldy who did some training, knew about this tree technique thing and bred whippets on the side.

Whenever anxiety takes hold and wants to blow me down, I imagine I am a tree; it stabilises me and makes me feel less anxious. I don't create a backstory to my tree; I don't decide that I'm a sixty-year-old downy birch in a field of wheat in the Cambridgeshire fens. I just imagine the roots coming through my shoes and making me feel better. But if it helps to embellish your tree, by all means do. You can give yourself a name, imagine what you look like, whether you have blossom in the spring and berries in the summer and, yes, if it helps, picture tree huggers latching onto your trunk.

It's the roots that are the important thing: the feeling of them balancing you, helping you feel more grounded. Go on – give it a go.

101

# 23. Complete small tasks

I have the cleanest, most frost-free freezer in the UK.

To be honest, it's probably the cleanest in Europe, and quite possibly the entire Northern Hemisphere. Because when anxiety comes, I defrost my freezer.

It's spotlessly clean and ice free. Seriously, come and look. I'm planning on doing paid tours in the near future. You'll get a free ice lolly with each admission.

Completing small tasks is really important when anxiety is hitting you. Your body is locked, so it's good to get unstuck. Your mind is telling you that you aren't capable of anything, so finishing something disproves that. Anxiety is telling you you're worthless, so you have to prove your worth by completing things. It sounds silly, but it totally works.

You have to make the task small and manageable. Trying to achieve world peace doesn't really cut it, I'm afraid; you'll have to do that some other time. I have a list of small tasks that I do when anxiety gets tough. These include folding my socks together, matching my socks together and buying socks online that my mother would call 'jazzy', but are simply different colours and patterns because boring socks are one of the worst things ever. Occasionally, when I have no sock-related tasks left, and my freezer is pristine, I reorganise my bookshelves, do some weeding in my garden and sort out my cutlery drawer.

103

When anxiety is at its peak, you don't want to do anything practical. You either want to flee or you want to freeze – and that's exactly why you should do the opposite, because anxiety is the reason God created a middle finger.

Other things I do include deleting old e-mails with a surly swipe of my thumb, smashing plates in the garden, trimming my beard (I concede not possible for everyone), brushing my cat's fur and cutting the dead leaves off my house plants. If you don't have any plants do this to your neighbours' hedge – I'm sure they'll be totally fine with that.

The other thing I want you to do is to notice that you are completing something as you do it. I want you to try and focus on the task, not on anxiety. Some people would call this mindfulness, but I don't; I just call it concentrating. If you feel inclined, you can do a running commentary in your head. I pretend to be a sports commentator.

'And he's off, he's got the scissors and has made the first trim of his beard beneath his chin. The Cisoria-Sibel 520 is a new brand of scissors for Withey and we're yet to see how effective they'll be – it's definitely a risk, but it might just pay off. You can see he's using his right little finger to steady himself, deviating from the more common ring-finger curl, so popular with the youngsters. Oh, wait, hang on – that's a mistake, he's gone deeper than he thought and lost a sizeable chunk to the right of his mouth. This is going to take skill and stamina to correct. Is he going to change scissors? I think he just might. Yes, there you go, as we thought, and he's gone for the EKS 19CG, perfect choice, he levels up the other side. Yes, YES! Beautifully done, you won't see many others with that kind of skill. Surely he will get the gold for this – and doesn't he look handsome now?'

I also do this when heating up a can of baked beans, pretending I have my own cookery programme.

'Welcome everyone. Today I'm making an ancient Slovenian peasant dish called beans on toast. So, I'm pouring the beans gently into a saucepan, just letting gravity do its work – that creates more aeration for the beans to infuse into the tomato juice. You may

need a wooden spoon to get the ones that stick to the
bottom of the can. Now, there are lots of views about
size and type of pan, but I go for a simple medium,
stainless steel. No doubt I'll get e-mails from you
cast-iron fanatics. Honestly, what are you like? But
I've made beans on toast a lot and this is what works
best for me.

'You need a slow rolling boil. I'm stirring every forty
seconds, this gives the beans optimum infusion time.
Anything less and you will have lukewarm beans.'

I think you get the idea. It distracts you and makes you
concentrate; then you realise that you're doing something
active; and at the end you have achieved something.

You probably have a list of small, easy-to-achieve jobs
that you've been putting off. Recently, when I was feeling
anxious, I painted over a stain on my sitting-room wall
where my cat had attacked it. It seems my cat thinks walls
are mice, an easy mistake to make. It's been staring at me,
ready to be painted, for months. Well OK, a year. Alright,
maybe two years. Fine, I'll admit it: FOUR WHOLE
YEARS. The feeling when I finally painted it over was
huge. It's what I call a 'mini gain': small, but massive for
my well-being – and a great way to manage your anxiety.

# 24. Goldilocks in da house

I have some good news and some bad news: you are never going to get rid of all your anxiety. That's both the good and the bad news, I'm afraid. Let me explain.

If you have eliminated all your anxiety, then no doubt you have somehow turned into a tranquilised manatee. Congratulations. For the rest of us, we carry on.

We need to learn how to worry with balance. We need to accept that there will always be some things that will make us anxious and try to be OK with that. It's all about how we react, and developing an appropriate response.

The aim is to get it about right, just like Goldilocks and her porridge (which is also supposed to be good for anxiety by the way). You don't want your anxiety spilling over and affecting your life; equally you don't want to be so laid-back that you turn into that drugged manatee. We need to get the balance as right as we can. A nice bowl of porridge, not too full, not too hot, not too cold, not too big, not too small. Some anxiety to keep us on our toes, but not so much that we get overly anxious and eat our toes.

It's OK to be anxious about starting a new job. It's appropriate to be nervous on your wedding day or when you're making a big presentation at work. Completely understandable to feel worried when a loved one is ill.

THE ACME
ANXOMETER

I want you to imagine a dial: it looks a bit like this. On the left-hand side are levels of anxiety that are completely natural. In the middle, where 12 would be on a clock face, is the dividing line. Everything on the right side is where anxiety is taking over. The plan is to try not to get over to the right-hand side.

When my anxiety goes to the right side, I can't sleep, I catastrophise, I seek constant reassurance, my anxiety multiplies, I lose my appetite, I don't want to speak to anyone, I don't want to go out and, when it's really bad, I get suicidal thoughts. In short, I feel utterly terrible. Have a think about what happens when your anxiety goes to the right side of the dial.

The problem with the right-hand side is that it's like Goldilocks eating the boiling hot porridge – it will hurt you. Basically, it's not good for your health. I'm sure you know all about the links between stress and physical illness; we need to protect ourselves as much as possible from this.

It's just like my fridge door (bear with me: this will make sense, I promise). I get anxious that I haven't closed the fridge door properly. This worries me on two accounts. Firstly because I think the fridge will start dripping, then flood the flat; and secondly, the food inside the fridge, which is mostly yoghurt to be fair, will go off and give me and Patrick food poisoning. I keep checking that the fridge door is shut. I've done this so much that the door has partly come off its hinges and doesn't really keep the food cool any more. My anxiety has hurt the fridge door; when anxiety creeps beyond the middle point of the dial, it hurts us too.

Now, being realistic, I know that sometimes my anxiety sneaks over to the other side of the dial. That's OK as long as I realise what's happening, don't beat myself up and do something about it. Trying is everything when it comes to the dial, so under no circumstances give yourself a hard time if it dips over. I will give you a very, very hard Paddington stare whenever you do this.

# 25. Try not to avoid things (don't skip this bit)

*Tuesday.*

I have to clean the bathroom. I hate cleaning the bathroom. It's my job to clean the bathroom but I hate cleaning the bathroom. I'll clean the bathroom tomorrow, I say to myself. I will definitely clean it tomorrow. Tomorrow will be a much better day to clean the bathroom because there will be more sunlight, and the sunlight will make it easier to see the dirt. In fact, why am I even considering cleaning the bathroom today when it's so dark? It's sheer madness to clean it today. Tomorrow is Wednesday and Wednesday is always a much better day for cleaning the bathroom as it's halfway through the week. Yes, that makes total sense. I will definitely do it tomorrow. Also, tomorrow I will have more energy to clean the bathroom because I will have slept better and it's a well-known fact that if you clean the bathroom with low energy then the germs breed faster and take over the whole room and then you have to clean even harder the next time. It's just logical to clean it tomorrow. Also, I don't have the best cleaning cloths for cleaning the bathroom; I only have cloths to clean the kitchen and they are totally different in every single way. Admittedly, they look alike, come from the same packet, come from the same manufacturer and have the same name, but the similarities end there. I will clean the bathroom tomorrow.

111

*Wednesday.*
Cut and paste the above paragraph, replacing 'Wednesday' with 'Thursday'.

Most of us try to avoid things that we don't like or make us feel worried. We put off the jobs that are more difficult to the last minute. With anxiety issues this is even more apparent, because why would we want to face something that is making us feel so much terror? Shall I try free-fall jumping from a plane at sixty thousand feet over Greenland or shall I do it another day? Tough question, eh?

The longer we avoid something, the harder it becomes to do and the larger it gets in our minds, hence why my bathroom remains unclean, occasionally, I suppose. Now avoidance isn't a problem if you don't need to jump out of a plane at sixty thousand feet but when it comes to meeting new people, making a presentation at work, going to a wedding by yourself or dealing with money worries, it's trickier to escape.

Sometimes – OK, often – I want to avoid life completely, head off to live alone on an island in the mid Pacific, eat fish and fruit and befriend a local dog called Bertie, but I've such a highly developed self-awareness that I've realised that this isn't realistic and is really just me wanting to avoid things. I know – I'm basically more enlightened than Buddha, aren't I? And the Dalai Lama is continually phoning me asking for advice about how to become more self-aware; it's like DL, man, enough already, leave me be.

Avoidance feeds anxiety, magnifies it and makes it worse. Anxiety wants you to avoid it so it can thrive; doing the opposite is always the way forward. Anxiety reduces when you gradually increase your exposure to what you're anxious about. Gradually is the key here – you can't go from being terrified of flying to piloting an Airbus A380 to Tahiti the following day.

My husband Patrick was terrified of flying. He couldn't even go to a conference in an airport, so great was his fear. No, he's not a jet fighter pilot now, it's not that kind of uplifting TED talk I'm afraid. When he was forced to fly to Amsterdam for work, he vomited every day for two weeks beforehand. When he did get to the Netherlands he phoned me to say the flight was so awful he was coming home on the train, boat or, if necessary, a passing mule.

So, we tackled it gradually, slowly, at a pace that was still scary but 'small steps are cool steps' – I've just made that up, but it totally works. We bought some hypnotherapy tapes, which he listened to for about three months, then we got a really short flight to Guernsey from Southampton – you basically go up in the air, they throw some peanuts at you, and then you come down again. Then we got a flight to Budapest the following year with the help of some Valium and a bottle of Belgian beer. Now he can fly up to about four hours, which is huge for him. The US or anywhere further afield isn't possible, but it's a massive achievement and was only possible because we did it gradually.

When we avoid something we're anxious about, initially it feels great, a huge relief. But you have to think long term, not short term, and to do that you need to tap into your motivation to make a change.

Patrick knew that if he was able to fly we would be able to go to places he'd always wanted to visit. It takes a while to get to the Arctic Circle by train (and he gets sick on boats) so with the amount of annual leave we have, we would get there, have enough time for a reindeer latte and immediately have to come back.

You can apply this principle to lots of activities that you're putting off. It will still feel scary and you'll still have to go gently, but if there's a nice reward at the end it makes it easier to do – and how frigging amazing are you going to feel when you've done it? The answer to that my friends, is REALLY frigging amazing , not least because you've kicked anxiety's butt in the process.

# 26. To be honest mate, you're not thinking straight

115

I'm running along by the sea having stormed out of the flat. My anxiety feels as if it's being expelled through my stomach like something in the film *Alien*.

I say running, but I'm actually just walking fast. If I run anywhere I get out of breath in a few seconds and look like a waddling, damp, bald penguin. I'm walking as quickly as I can because now that anxiety has escaped through my stomach, it's following me and is going to attack me with an electric hedge trimmer. If I keep running, maybe I can escape it.

My husband has tried to get me to talk, to sit down, to rest, to sleep or to stay in the flat where I'm safe. I think I know better and, in my head, walking barefoot, penguin-like by the sea at 2 a.m. in November, in the rain, is the best option.

I have no idea where I'm going.

Patrick phones. I ignore him and keep walking. I'm

heading east for some reason. I guess it's good that I'm not walking south, into the sea. Of course, the rain is hitting me in the face, which means I can't see anything because I wear glasses, so I accidently bang into a lamp-post and bash my knee. If it wasn't so awful, looking at this scene from above would make for great slapstick comedy. Buster Keaton has nothing on me.

'Just come home, James,' texts Patrick. I ignore that too. I have to keep walking/waddling. I have to escape anxiety.

Looking back at this, I can see how my mind wasn't in the right space. I'm unwell. My ability to make good decisions and reason things out has been massively impacted. Let's be honest, walking without shoes when it's soaking wet and 2 degrees Celsius in the middle of the night is not the best thing to do. It is definitely not the best thing to do to manage anxiety, unless you're a penguin, maybe, and I'm not 100 per cent convinced I am a penguin.

It's like being in a dark tunnel trying to get to the exit. You keep going and going, hoping that the tunnel will end, and no train will come. Someone – Patrick in my case – is telling you there are doors to the side that'll help you get out faster, but you don't believe them, so you carry on despite the risk of Thomas the Tank Engine (and possibly Gordon too) coming down the track.

When our anxiety is high, we don't think straight. It's as simple as that. Our thinking is skewed because of the feelings we're having.

Patrick and I have a street cat who adopted us a few years ago. One day he came into the living room, sat on the sofa, started meowing for food and has basically never left. He's a nervous sort of fellow, having spent his first year fending for himself when he was abandoned by his owners. People are shits, they really are. He's terrified of being left alone in case he's abandoned again. In the first few weeks he used to follow me up the road to the train station when I headed out in the morning. Now, my employer would probably not have been OK with me bringing my cat to work – and I don't know how you teach your cat about train etiquette – but my cat wasn't thinking straight. His anxiety was so huge that he just wanted to be with me, and frankly who can blame him, he's only human . . .

When my anxiety comes, I think of my cat and how his behaviour is influenced by his anxious thoughts. This helps me calm myself down and think more rationally. Developing an awareness – and then remembering – that we're not thinking straight when we're anxious is the key here. As with many other things, I have this written on my phone as a reminder: 'James, when you're feeling anxious you won't be thinking straight'. It's not a quote to match any of the lines of Martin Luther King Jr's 'I have a dream' speech, but it gives me the insight I need to take time to think about what I'm doing and not just react and end up making wrong and frankly bizarre decisions.

If all else fails, I eat some catnip, open a can of tuna and kick back with my knitted mouse.

# 27. Soothe to remove

I have a list of soothing activities for when I become anxious that lessen my feelings of anxiety – it's the equivalent of a children's comfort blanket.

One of the things I do is to listen to soothing Germanic operatic arias sung by sopranos. I have no idea what they're singing about. For all I know they could be rhapsodising about mass homicide. 'And then I killed seventy hundred and fifty people with a large, serrated sword. One man died when, unfortunately, both his kidneys fell out.' I really haven't a clue.

I know absolutely nothing about opera. I have seen two live productions in my lifetime because my husband wanted to go. The first one was in France on our first trip abroad together. I suppose, wanting to impress my then boyfriend with my linguistic skills, I said I would go into the Paris Opera House and get some cheap tickets in the gods. Now, my French has never been great; I managed to scrape a pass at school, but that's it. This is how the conversation went, albeit in French.

ME: Good morning. [*It was 7 p.m.*] I am an English woman.

WOMAN: Good evening. [*Starts giggling*]

ME: Yes, err . . . good night. I demand tickets for yesterday.

WOMAN: Of course.

ME: Yes. I want *very* expensive tickets.

WOMAN: *Very* expensive tickets sir? [*Openly laughing*]

ME: Ummm . . . Yes, *very* expensive tickets.

WOMAN: You are sure you want *very* expensive tickets?

ME: Who? How many? Good afternoon. What? Yes, *very* expensive.

WOMAN: [*Now joined by two colleagues, also laughing*] Of course sir. [*Hands me tickets and is now on floor laughing with colleagues*]

ME: I am thanking you lady please.

WOMAN: Goodbye, enjoy the opera.

ME: See you soon, my sweetheart. [*Go outside to meet Patrick; we speak in English*]

120

PATRICK: How did you get on?

ME: Well, they were laughing for some reason, bit rude to be honest, I know my French is a little bit rusty, but I was really trying. I got the cheap tickets though.

PATRICK: [*Checks remaining money*] You've . . . you've . . . I can't believe it, you've just spent £200 on these tickets!

ME: What? I can't have, I asked for the cheapest.

And that's how we ended up in the royal box at the Paris Opera House.

Anyway, one of the opera singers performed the most beautiful song – possibly about genocide, who knows – and I found myself relaxing. Who cared that we were wearing ripped jeans and had two huge rucksacks in the royal box? Who cared that people with diamond tiaras were giving us daggers from the stalls? Who cared that the person inspecting the tickets asked if we had mistaken the Paris Opera House for the nearby homeless shelter? It was all lovely and I didn't care.

It doesn't matter that I don't understand opera, know nothing about composers, orchestras or how people actually make that sort of warbling sound. All that matters is that it helps me.

Other things I do include curling up under a tartan blanket and watching cosy crime dramas on TV, the more poorly acted the better. I light an incense stick – call me an old hippy if you want, but I find certain smells very relaxing, plus it means I can pretend I'm in a Moroccan hammam being infused with spices I can neither spell nor pronounce.

Create your own list of things that help you. I call mine the 'Soothing Selection' because it sounds like a radio station's late-night Sunday evening programme, hosted by someone called Bernie.

You have to experiment a bit, as not everything will work. If incomprehensible German opera doesn't work for you (and I won't be offended if it doesn't), then try downloading the relaxing mating call of the Australian channel-billed cuckoo.

# 28. Find your blowholes

I'm at work and I've run to the toilet, but not for the usual ablutions.

Anxiety is pumping through my blood and seeping out of my skin pores. I shut the toilet door and struggle to breathe properly. If anyone comes in now – and in all honesty I'm not sure I've locked the door properly, so it's a possibility – they'll see a bald, middle-aged, bespectacled, sweating man, panting and crouching like he was in the last stages of childbirth. Not at my most alluring, it has to be said.

Suddenly, in the midst of this anxiety madness, a picture of a whale comes to mind, blowing out water into the sea, goodness knows why. To try and calm myself down, and because I can't think of anything better to do, I pretend I have blowholes in the side of my head. It seems to help. With each breath, I blow out the anxiety though my imaginary holes (steady now). I have to get it out. Inside it's doing me no good. Get the anxiety out.

Many experts on anxiety talk about the importance of breathing, things like counting to ten slowly and regulating your breath. All this is definitely important and can work really well. But now, when anxiety hits, I become a whale. OK, don't judge me quite yet; read to the end, then judge me.

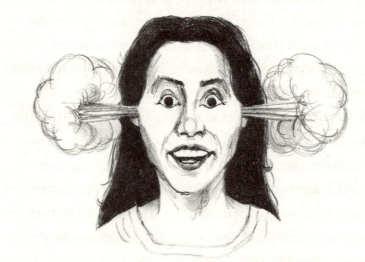

When whales come to the surface they blow out air from holes in their heads. They need to do this in order to survive. And yes, thank you, I know that not all whales have two holes and they are not usually on the sides of their heads, and I know (because I looked it up) that it's called a spiracle, but you get the general idea.

The more you practise this technique, the easier it becomes to manage the pain. Have a look on the internet first to see how the whales do it. Type in 'Whales blowing out water', watch their vigour and control and then copy that. It's better if you can search for a humpback whale because firstly, they have two holes, and secondly, it's a funny name. Google it now. I'll be here when you get back.

Did you have a look? Marvellous, isn't it? With each blow, anxiety will be forcibly ejected from your head and dispersed into the air. You can also make a blowing sound by puckering your lips and making them vibrate. This works especially well if you've had 30ml of lip filler injected into you, but even if you haven't it's still worth a try.

Imagination is as strong as memory. Using your imagination to expel anxiety from blowholes on the side of your head may sound silly, but when anxiety impacts on us it's such an odd feeling anyway that using something equally weird can really help.

Whales have developed a perfect survival skill, and by using this technique we can learn to live too.

125

# 29. You're YOU, not your anxiety

My anxiety is like one of those basking sharks – you know the ones with huge mouths that just gulp water and hope that there's some plankton in there somewhere. It consumes me. It doesn't care about swallowing everything and destroying my life in the process. It has cost me jobs, friendships, relationships and acres of wasted time I could have used to studiously research the resilient properties of *Noctiluca scintillans* (that's plankton).

What I hate most about anxiety is how it robs me of myself, how it overtakes me, how it tries to rule my life.

Severe anxiety is a part of me, as is my depression, but it's not the sum total of me. I won't be defined by it, but neither am I ashamed of it. I am James, I have anxiety, but I am not my anxiety. I accept that I have it, I accept that I will always struggle with it, but I'm also going to fight back. And I do a mean cancan-like high kick.

Having a diagnosis of anxiety was really helpful

because it legitimised all the stuff in my head that I'd assumed was just me being weird – but that didn't mean I was going to change my name to James 'Anxiety' Withey.

One of the ways of fighting back is to separate yourself from the anxiety. This keeps anxiety in check, so we can see it for what it is and ensure that it doesn't infest us with shame.

There is already enough that we can't control – governments we didn't vote for, rises in taxes just to line the pockets of politicians' friends, exorbitant train fares, dictators wearing stupid hats threatening to blow up the world, idiots killing wild animals for 'sport' and the travesty that is squeezable Marmite – so let's make a concerted effort not to let anxiety add to the crap fest.

To ensure we put anxiety in its right place, we have to make sure we remember all the other things we are: our values, our beliefs, our passions, our personality. All of these things whip anxiety's arse.

When I'm struggling and feel like a plankton being swallowed by that damn shark, I repeat the following (I've written it down obviously; my memory is terrible).

'I like yoghurt. I like walking by the sea. I like cats and dogs and sloths and elephants. I like art. I like gardens and gardening. I like old houses. I like cheesy TV and cheesy food. I like travelling. I like cocktails. I like the theatre. I don't like being horrible to people. I believe in championing people who have been trampled on, and those who do the trampling can kiss my smelly toes. Oh, I also like pizza, reading, second-hand bookshops, talking about books, giving book presents, going to book talks. And, most of all, Marmite is my religion, but don't make me squeeze it.'

You can do your own list, but feel free to pinch any of mine if you want. Let it be a mantra to ground yourself when anxiety takes over. It is a picture of who you are, and it's far stronger and more important than your anxiety.

# 30. Respond, don't react

I'm on a train to the airport to catch a flight to Ireland, where I'm spending the weekend with a friend and Patrick, who are both already there. I've left loads of time to get there, literally hours, because I'm always so worried about being late. Fifteen minutes into the twenty-minute journey, the train breaks down.

It's fine, I tell myself, I've got loads of time to spare, not a problem. I can read my book, take in the scenery – though admittedly it's a zone of light industry in the middle of nowhere – and relax knowing that being early has finally paid off. It also means I'm not sat at the airport for hours looking around the duty-free shop for the thirteenth time, perfecting a kind of duck-and-move gesture usually only seen in professional rugby as I try not to be sprayed with perfume by the overzealous shop assistant.

Except the train doesn't move after a few minutes as I'd hoped. The dreaded 'bing bong' of the tannoy rings out.

'I'm sorry to inform you that a cow has fallen asleep on

the line – or it might be dead, we're not sure – anyway, it's in the way and we're just waiting for the farmer to come and get it.'

Fine, I thought, fine. The farmer probably lives nearby, they'll come, move the cow, however you move a cow, and we will be on our way.

Twenty minutes pass. Bing bong.

'Unfortunately, it seems that the farmer is away on holiday, in Zakynthos. We think that's an island in Greece, but we're waiting for confirmation. So, a neighbouring farmer is coming to help instead. Sorry for the delay.'

An hour passes. Now I'm starting to panic. If the cow is moved in the next half hour, can I still catch the flight? Maybe the cow will move by itself. Maybe someone needs to put a carrot in front of it. Does that work for cows, or is it only donkeys and horses? Maybe I should get out, buy a carrot from a local supermarket and put it in the cow's face.

In a panic, I spring up, go to the door and try to open it with my hand, but it won't move. Bugger! If I can't get out, how can I get the carrot to the cow? Now we will never get to the airport and I'll miss my flight, and everything will be a disaster. I try to wrench the door open with both hands, but it still won't budge. Bugger, bugger, bugger! Now a woman is looking at me like I'm a mad man, which I am, but still, it's a bit rude. I start hammering on the button, but it doesn't release the door. I swear loudly and sit down again, sweating. Bugger it.

Bing bong.

'Sorry for the ongoing delay to this service caused by a cow on the line. It's a Holstein Friesian, if you're interested, originally from Schleswig-Holstein in Northern Germany. The neighbouring farmer was on his way but unfortunately his 4x4 vehicle has broken down. They're not built to last these British engines, that's the problem. He should have bought a Toyota; I find them very reliable, I've had mine for twelve years and it's never given me a moment of worry. You are entitled to a free hot beverage and a brie and cress sandwich, but unfortunately there's no trolley service on this train. However we are coming round handing out vouchers that you can redeem for a 25g cereal bar at your local newsagent.'

My heart is beating so fast I fear it will leap out of my jumper. I open the window and try to lean out but it's one of those long, slim ones and I can't get my head through. I've no idea *why* I'm trying to lean out of the window. Perhaps, the cow will see me glaring at it and think, *Now, that's a man in a hurry, I will move and let him catch flight 186 to Dublin International Airport.*

God, I hate cows. Confirmed pescatarian that I am, I would happily see this particular one cut up for ancho steak with chimichurri buttered sweetcorn for being so stupid. Who falls asleep on a railway line? Honestly, find a nice divan bed like everyone else.

Eventually, the farmer's friend came with a large stick, the cow got up, farted and went into the next field. The train restarted and I, of course, missed my flight and had to pay £40,000 for another one. Well, it felt like £40,000. It all ended OK, though: I had a great time in Ireland, I didn't eat any revenge steak, and all was well.

When I look back at this, I can see how I reacted badly, especially the part where I wanted the cow killed. I was reacting with my anxiety, not my rational brain. Admittedly, my rational brain is often hard to find anyway, but I can see what I should have done differently. By reacting with my anxiety, I tried to open the train doors with my bare hands, tried to escape to buy a carrot for a cow and tried to put my head through a tiny window.

I didn't think of all the sensible stuff that I should have done had I *responded* to my anxiety rather than *reacting* to it. Does that make sense? If I had responded to feeling anxious about missing my flight, I would have phoned Patrick to tell him what was going on, got some support and advice from him, phoned the airline to ask them what I could do, when the next flight would be, how much a new ticket would cost and so on. Most importantly, I would not have leapt around the train like a springer spaniel on cheap cocaine on a large bouncy castle. I achieved nothing apart from making myself more anxious and exhausted. I couldn't control the train, I couldn't control the cow and I couldn't control when the flight left. Sometimes I have to remind myself I am not God. Who knew?

When we *respond* rather than *react*, we tap into the part of our mind that sees anxiety as a useless emotion; it doesn't help us, it just blinds and binds us. When a situation like this arises, I play two versions of a short, animated film in my head. The first film is me on the train, rushing around, panicking, buying carrots, thinking I can open closed doors and so on. The second is a much calmer me, frustrated and worried but being more rational, calling my husband, calling the airline and accepting that I don't have special powers to make a cow moo-ve (sorry). This is the version of events I try to emulate. I suspect you've had a similar experience when you've reacted rather than responded, and you too can create your own short film as a prompt. There, now you're a film producer.

The next part of this is to play a film in your head of the situation you're in, but do it when it arises, in the present moment. For example, maybe you've just been given some feedback from your boss about how to improve a part of your job. You could play the film that shows you crying in the toilet, telling yourself you're worthless and expect to be sacked the next day. Or you could take a breath, and play the film where you respond calmly, ask your boss questions about anything you don't understand and write down the answers, knowing that if you're getting feedback that doesn't mean imminent unemployment.

Go for it, Spielberg.

# 31. You're talkin' to me?

Anxiety would love us not to talk about it, then it can fester like a bubbling yeast product in our stomachs, the spores flinging themselves free and spreading to the rest of our body.

When I first started seeing a counsellor about my anxiety, I didn't really know how it would help, and I was massively anxious about going in the first place. I was in such a state that anything would set off my anxious thoughts, but I knew I needed to do something.

I managed to find someone I could open up to, who I could trust and who didn't judge my obsession with worrying whether someone would fall and break their neck if I left some drops of water on the floor of a public toilet. He was also OK with my worries around leaving the house, being sacked from work for being a duffus and my incredible superpower of looking at people and them dying. He was earning his money.

Before our first meeting, I was so anxious that I would

misinterpret every word he said and somehow use it as more evidence of me being a Super Duffus (Level 2 on the Withey-Duffus Scale – when you reach Level 10, Grand Master Duffus, you get a jaunty sash and a lifetime supply of tranquilisers). But over time, having someone who listened, understood and didn't judge me meant that I could look at my anxiety, uncover some of the reasons for it – childhood bereavement, loss of control, anger, abuse and lots of other lovely, fluffy stuff – and find a way of managing it and living my life.

A lot of anxiety issues are treated with cognitive behavioural therapy (CBT), which is not to be confused with compulsory basic training to ride a motorbike (also called CBT). I can't believe no one has combined the two, to be honest; therapy on a motorbike could be the new thing.

Cognitive behavioural therapy allows you to look at your thoughts, beliefs and feelings and how they impact on your behaviour. It works really well for some people with anxiety. I've had it myself and some of the techniques helped. My suggestion would be to find a CBT therapist who combines it with a compassionate approach. Don't worry if CBT doesn't work for you; the most important thing is to find a qualified counsellor who you trust and can open up to about your anxiety. My current counsellor isn't a CBT therapist and their way of working is just as useful with my anxiety issues.

Of course, you needn't limit yourself to speaking only to a counsellor. Friends and relatives can do a great job too, but don't expect them to perform the same role as a counsellor. Be aware that they might say things that hurt, however well-intentioned they are.

Anxiety is probably telling you that you're not worthy of having any help. But if you're not worthy of help, then who is? The person next door who keeps Russian hamsters? Your work colleague who has a penchant for grilled-sardine-and-egg-mayonnaise open sandwiches at lunch-time? Your cousin who once laughed so much while eating trifle that jelly came out of their nose?

137

I have news: we're all worthy of help, especially YOU right now. Yes, really, and anytime you doubt it I want you to picture me staring at you over my glasses and pointing a Sherlock Holmes pipe in your direction. Anxiety makes us hate ourselves and doubt ourselves, so listen to me and not it.

The other technique I use when I think I'm not worthy of support is to imagine all those people on helplines and web chats waiting for me to contact them. They want to help. They want to listen.

Saying things out loud is healing. I don't know why – I once heard it's something to do with cortisol levels – but in truth it doesn't really matter; what matters is that it helps.

Your anxiety may be related to a specific trauma that

you need to look at. Sometimes we can trace the roots of our anxiety back to something that happened in our childhood, or to another point in our life. Sometimes our anxiety is a relic of the person that we were years ago, but the anxiety has continued. Sometimes there isn't anything specific – it's just part of who we are. So don't be worrying if you can't trace your anxiety back to that time when you were eight and an emu mugged you in the street, and now even the merest glimpse of an emu makes you feel sick with worry.

Talking to other people who have anxiety too – the fancy name is peer support networks – can be incredibly helpful because we 'get' each other's feelings. We understand that things that may seem small to others can make us 'anxiety-ites' curl up with fear. Also, we can ask others what they do, what makes it easier for them.

# 32. Distract: do one thing

One of the ways that I manage my anxiety, and the endless exasperating background rumination that accompanies it, is to distract myself.

It's hard to focus on two things at once, so if I'm engaged in one activity it takes my mind off the impending doom scenario that anxiety is promising me. I've tried lots of distractions and have discovered the ones that work best for me.

I watch terrible television, mostly old *Real Housewives* programmes featuring rich, self-obsessed people arguing about plastic surgery, how to furnish their fifty-thousand-square-foot mansion, and which dog will match their Chanel shopping bag. The frivolous, inconsequential nature of it all takes my head to somewhere so completely different from my own anxiety that the doom-ridden thoughts start to ebb away. The trick here is that it's got to be trash TV, but quality trash: look for good production values to keep you invested, but subject matter that is essentially vapid so that your concentration levels aren't too taxed. Yes, I have thought A LOT about this and have found the perfect combination.

When I'm in a full-blown anxiety attack, I do exercises that require more application. I will use the alphabet to name my most hated dead famous people by their first name e.g., A for Adolf Hitler; that's an easy one to start with. I freely admit this is a terrible, terrible thing to do when I've never even met them, but somehow anger, wrath and judging people works – and, hey, who doesn't like starting a hate list with Hitler? Give it a try. It's totally fine to do this in your head (and they'll never know).

If you want to be more cerebral about things, you could try naming Pulitzer Prize-winning book titles, or nineteenth-century Scandinavian philosophers, or Nobel prize winners between 1959 and 1962. If you want to join me in my shallowness, you can try your most hated politicians, most hated celebrities (I *love* doing this), most hated food and so on. Whenever I'm reciting my food list and I get to T, for tripe, I scream really loudly, like you do when you're singing 'five gold rings' in 'The Twelve Days of Christmas'. Seriously, ban tripe now – it's even more vile than anxiety.

Distraction also allows time for your anxiety to calm the feck down. Remember anxiety usually peaks and then decreases, like cravings and anger. It won't always stay at the height of the terror, and while you're doing something else it can peak and then dip.

You can read books, read magazines, play computer games, go for a hike, clean your house, garden, binge watch a Netflix series, cycle, paint, knit, go for a drive, walk the dog. You have to keep experimenting to find the right things that work. It took me a lot of time to discover my petty and superficial distraction techniques. I had to watch a lot of trashy television before I found what suited me, but I was surprisingly good at it; it's amazing the skills you can add to your CV.

141

# 33. On getting reassurance and putting on your pants

A conversation with my husband about my new job.

ME: Do you think this job is right for me?

HIM: I don't know, what do you think?

ME: Maybe it is – or maybe I've made the wrong decision? Do you think I've made the wrong decision? What do you think?

HIM: You'll just have to see how it goes.

ME: God, maybe I've made a mistake. What if I've made a mistake? Is it a massive, massive mistake?

HIM: You won't know until you start, James.

ME: It will be alright, won't it?

HIM: I hope so, but I don't know.

ME: What if it's not the right job? What do I do then?

HIM: Then we'll sort it out.

ME: It will be OK, won't it? I mean, do you think it will all be fine?

HIM: You'll have to wait and see.

ME: But what do you think? Have I made a mistake?

HIM: I'm not a mind-reader – I don't know if it's a mistake.

ME: What do I do if I've made a mistake?

HIM: As I've said, we'll manage it if it happens.

ME: So, you think it *will* happen?

HIM: I didn't say that. I said, if it turns out it isn't the right job for you, then we will tackle it then.

ME: It will be OK, won't it?

This conversation went around in circles for the next hour, and then for another hour the following day. And the following day. And, yes, the following day too.

Anxiety plays on some of our most human fears: of dying, being ill, being alone, being accused, being judged, being without money, being humiliated, being imprisoned, being homeless, being hungry, being unemployed and being bereaved. It's therefore natural that we seek reassurance from others when our anxiety is high.

The trouble is, getting reassurance is like continuing to cycle into a headwind – at some point you need to go the other way to make the ride easier. Excessive reassurance can be damaging as it prevents us from being able to manage day-to-day anxieties by ourselves. It becomes obsessive, addictive and exhausting.

When my anxiety is high and I can't make any decisions without reassurance, it renders me immobile and dependent on others. When this happens, I put on my big anti-anxiety pants. They're fabulous, complete with sequins that sparkle like a carnival headdress at Mardi Gras, and they fit perfectly. These are of course metaphorical pants, but feel free to fashion some actual anti-anxiety pants if you have those particular haberdashery skills. Embellish them with your favourite football team, manga character or film star – anything that gives you strength, folks.

When I put them on, I take a deep breath, feel the power in the pants (stop laughing) and summon up all the courage I can muster. I'm not a big one for positive affirmations but there are always exceptions, and when I put the pants on I simply say, 'Come on, you can do this.' That's it. Nothing too grandiose.

I get gratification from having dealt with the situation myself and not having asked anyone for reassurance. I gently preserve this in my memory, when no one can touch it, so I remember that good feeling and can use it for next time. The more you can recall that feeling, the more you want to get that feeling and the easier it is to manage the anxiety without excessive reassurance.

You have to do this in stages (not the pants – the pants you can put on right away). Just build up slowly, dealing with smaller anxieties first. I started by tackling my anxiety around used matches – I was anxious they might magically relight and burn the flat down. I put on my pants, took a deep breath and said to myself, 'You've checked the match is out twice, it's in the sink, it can't self-combust. Come on, you can do this.' I then went and sat in the living room (admittedly still feeling anxious and desperate to check the match again).

145

But when time passed – and the kitchen wasn't on fire – I was very pleased with myself. I had evidence that: a) matches don't spontaneously relight, and b) I could manage the anxiety by myself. Things grew from there, and I can still recall that initial wonderful feeling of pride for managing it without seeking help.

Of course, I absolutely do not need any reassurance that you're liking this book. Not at all. No. But, I mean, you are, aren't you? Yes? Please tell me you are. E-mail me, direct message me, text me, send a note via carrier pigeon to say how much you're loving it.

Bugger.

Better put my sparkly pants on.

# 34. A word about the drugs

I'm on the phone to my friend, trying to get advice about how to calm my anxiety.

> FRIEND: Have you tried having a hot bath?
>
> ME: Yes.
>
> FRIEND: Have you tried a hot bath with a lavender and valerian bath bomb?
>
> ME: Yes.
>
> FRIEND: Have you tried a hot bath with a lavender and valerian bath bomb and some narwhal music?
>
> ME: Yes.
>
> FRIEND: Have you tried a hot bath with a lavender and valerian bath bomb, some narwhal music and a mug of lemon balm tea?
>
> ME: Yes.
>
> FRIEND: Have you tried a hot bath with a lavender and

valerian bath bomb, some narwhal music, a mug of lemon balm tea and a passion flower tablet?

ME: Yes.

FRIEND: Have you tried–

ME: [*Puts phone down*]

I'm happy to give anything a go if it helps my anxiety. Seriously, sign me up for koala cuddling, Albanian worry-bead-making or sensuous seaweed-body-wrapping – bring it all on. It doesn't always work, though, particularly as the availability of koalas willing to be cuddled is limited in my part of the UK, so sometimes, when things are really bad, I have to take medication.

I take pills for my depression. I take medication for my stomach. Sometimes I take tablets for insomnia, as well as iron and vitamin D supplements. My medicine cabinet spits everything out every few months through sheer exhaustion. We don't do pill-shaming in my house – only idiots do that – and, if your doctor advises it, it's fine to take medication for things if you need to. Without it, we'd be far worse off, perhaps even dead, which would be a bit of a bummer.

I'm prescribed Valium when I need it, which is when my anxiety is really, really terrible. When you first go to your doctor, they might prescribe beta blockers, or anti-depressants or benzodiazepines (which are like Valium). It all depends on your circumstances and what the doctor thinks is the best option for you. Many medications are prescribed to help you to think more clearly, as severe anxiety reduces your ability to function.

The thing about taking any medication is that you have to be very clear what the positive *and* potentially negative effects are. If your doctor doesn't talk about side effects, possible dependence and how long you should take them, then please ask them. If you don't get a satisfactory answer, go to another doctor. You need to have a clear picture of the drug you're being given.

Now, a word about alcohol (another drug, I'm afraid). It can be easy to reach for a drink when our anxiety is high as it *seems* to make us more confident. A word of warning, though: alcohol doesn't make us more confident; it just makes us care less, which is very different. Think about it for a second. You've had a few drinks at a wedding because you don't know anybody, and things have gone swimmingly because you've cared less about what happens and what others think of you. But the next day you're not feeling more confident, and your anxiety hasn't gone . . . I guess what I'm saying is, alcohol isn't the answer to managing your anxiety in the long term. By all means, do have a drink – I'm a sucker for a good cocktail myself – but always in moderation and never as a coping mechanism for your anxiety.

The other thing to note is that no medication for mental health is a cure-all. It is better when taken alongside some talking therapies and support – so combine this chapter with Chapter 31. I thank you.

# 35. Triggers (not gun-related)

Hi, I'm Julie Andrews, Hollywood legend and star of the award-winning 1965 film, *The Sound of Music*. Here are a few of my triggering things.

The *Six O'Clock News*. Cooking for people. Going to parties with people who like to talk about nuclear physics. Sitting next to grumpy strangers at weddings. Shopping for clothes. Shopping for shoes. Shopping for food. Looking at myself in a full-length mirror. Dealing with stupid idiots on public transport. Being off sick from work. Getting things wrong at work. Being late. Unwanted noise from neighbours. Thinking I have offended people. Feeling out of control. Feeling embarrassed. Worrying that I've left the cooker on. Worrying that the washing machine will explode. Worrying that *I* will explode. Thinking that I've put on weight. Worrying that the house will be burgled when I go on holiday. My family being ill. My friends being ill. My cat being ill. Me being ill. Thinking that I've hurt people. And, most of all, those well-meaning charity adverts of abandoned sad donkeys.

Yes, I know it doesn't rhyme or scan like the actual song in the film – and anyway, that was called 'My Favorite Things' – but who do you think I am, Oscar Hammerstein?

These are some of the things that trigger my anxiety. You can e-mail me for a comprehensive list if you'd like one, but I warn you it goes on for seventy-four pages, double-sided, in a very small font.

There are lots of things that don't make me anxious, of course. I just can't think of any at the moment. No, wait – OK, eating yoghurt doesn't make me anxious – unless it's been secretly infused with poison by my ex-boyfriend who has covertly infiltrated the dairy factory for the sole purpose of killing me. Why are you looking at me like that? I keep telling you – I will *always* win the 'Who's the most weird?' competition.

The truth is there are some things I can do that don't make me as anxious as other things. Public speaking, for example. For some reason, I can do it and not have a full-on breakdown afterwards, which is how I categorise 'manageable anxiety'. Also, I'm happy to pee in public toilets. Let's move on, shall we? It's probably for the best.

My cat has numerous anxiety triggers, but his biggest is his arch nemesis 'Señor Nasty Cat' (possibly not his real name) coming to eat his food. He insists on us checking out the mean streets with him to ensure that Señor Nasty Cat, or SNC to his homies, is not invading his territory.

We all have different triggers, and being aware of them means you can tackle, avoid or manage them. Many people will say you always need to tackle anxiety head-on rather than avoid your triggers, but this is true only for *some* things, such as the triggers that really impact negatively on you and stop you from living your life. Other stuff you can happily avoid. I limit my news intake; once a day is quite enough. I turn the channel over when the sad donkeys are on. It doesn't mean I don't care – I often make a donation to donkey charities – but for some reason the TV programmes I watch *always* have adverts with sad donkeys, so I have to limit my intake otherwise I would be crying and worrying about sad donkeys all day.

Other triggers I examine with the help of a professional in counselling. I have come to realise a lot of my anxiety is about feeling out of control, and relates to when my dad died when I was five years old, on Christmas Day of all days – how selfish was that? I mean, dude, just choose, like, any other day. Being aware of this helps me understand my anxiety and then manage it. The reason that I worry about killing people is because as a child I felt responsible for my dad's death. I also blame Father Christmas and Rudolph especially, but I'm only just starting to examine this; at the moment it's just an i-deer.

I don't apologise for the appalling joke above.

# 36. Feed yourself, not your anxiety

153

 I'm on a flight to Venice with Patrick. It's 4.30 a.m. because I've stupidly bought cheap tickets, and now I'm cursing myself for being a skinflint and having only had three hours' sleep. The airport we're flying into is so far away from Venice it's actually in northern Ukraine. I'm gulping a bottle of sludge that I bought from a café because it was green, and I thought it would be good for me.

Suddenly, I start to feel anxious. I'm usually OK on planes; it's Patrick who hates flying, so I feel doubly weird. Then my heart starts beating faster and I'm squirming in my seat. What on earth is happening? All of a sudden I want to smash the window to get out, but I've read somewhere that you're not allowed to do that at thirty-eight thousand feet, so I just sit there feeling worse and worse, while Patrick sleeps.

We land at the airport, with my anxiety increasing, and wait for the train to Venice. On the platform an old Italian man says something to us – in Italian, obviously – and it wasn't 'cappuccino' so I've no idea what he said. For some reason, I take his comment to be a threat or abuse or something, so I charge after him. I have no idea what I'm going to do when I actually get to him. Patrick quickly grabs me and holds me back like a pleading girlfriend with her aggressive boyfriend wanting a fight in a club.

'What the hell are you doing, James? Get back here. You can't fight a ninety-year-old man.'

'I know he's old, but he insulted me.'

'The reason you can't fight a ninety-year-old man is because he'll beat you to a pulp, you weak southern plonker, plus all he said to you was "Good morning". What's the matter with you – and what the hell was in that disgusting-looking green sludge drink?'

We checked. It contained 80mg of caffeine. Now, Patrick can down six double espressos in a row and still be calm, sleep well and generally be pretty passive about stuff. Give me one tiny, itsy-bitsy sip of coffee and my anxiety will hit the roof faster than a cheetah on a running machine. I won't sleep for the next fourteen nights. I'll worry about whether carrots have feelings, if my cat is being too co-dependent and about the possibility of the world imploding next November. In addition, I now apparently look for fights with elderly Italian men at train stations. That will be the fight bit of the 'fight or flight' response, I guess.

Similarly, alcohol is really bad for my anxiety. It's OK when I'm drinking it, but the next day I feel horrendous. All my anxieties seem to accumulate, expand and take me over. I still have a drink, but the next day I remember the anxious thoughts are caused by the alcohol and I spend a few hours under my duvet.

I've also found certain foods seem to impact on my anxiety; unfortunately it's all the stuff that tastes great and is full of sugar. I think this is to do with having a big sugar rush and then crashing. I tend to stay away from chocolate, cakes and high-sugar stuff, but, listen, you don't need to go full-on puritan and only eat soup made with nettles plucked from the hedgerows. Just know that what you put into your tummy can make your anxiety worse.

Anxiety can also impact on your appetite, either decreasing it or increasing it. My appetite disappears, I feel sick and I don't want to eat a thing, which undoubtedly makes things worse as my brain isn't getting the nourishment it needs to help it think more clearly. When my friend Dylan gets anxious, he hoovers up everything in the fridge and then goes out to the corner shop to buy more. Both of these practices make anxiety worse.

What I do is have some nutrition drinks in the cupboard, and when I'm feeling anxious I guzzle one of those as it's got all the things my body needs (and also means I don't need to cook).

# 37. Nature and all that lovely stuff

It's a grim, January-ish sort of day – which is appropriate, as it's January.

My anxiety is poking me with a stick – I worry about work, I worry about the cat's sticky eye, I worry about the giant pandas not breeding and my plants not growing. If I let this go on long enough, I will be up all night anxious about Norma from Campbell Creek, Wyoming, whose garden is infested with chipmunks. What if they get into her house and start eating it from the inside? What if they poo in her kitchen and she gets some sort of chipmunk poo disease? I don't even know Norma. I'm sure she's lovely, but I shouldn't be worrying about her chipmunk problem.

I head to the sea which is handily placed at the bottom of my road – very nice of it to be so near. And, yes, I do know how lucky I am. There was a huge storm last night and the waves are enormous. The big waves merge with smaller ones for greater impact, then announce themselves on the beach with unfiltered aggression. It's wondrous, utterly humbling and energising. I sit on the beach, as near to the waves as I safely can, and the spray hits me in the face. I start to feel a bit better.

I'm definitely a sea sort of person. It does something to me. The waves are constant, and yet they're constantly changing. I love looking out at something that will be here long after I'm gone. Soothing is probably the word that best describes how I feel when I head to the sea.

157

It is well documented that being in nature helps anxiety. It's not as simple as 'go for a walk in the mountains' if mountains don't soothe you, which they don't me; I just feel claustrophobic. Also, if you don't have any mountains nearby it makes things slightly more difficult. It's a case of finding what sort of outdoor space works best for you. Take me to a bleak moor and I want to flee back to the city instantly, but for some people it's just the tonic they need.

I like walking with huge trees overhead. Not the spooky canopy of a dark forest, but a great arboretum with vast, mature trees really works wonders. I like finding my favourite tree, searching for pleasing branch shapes, connecting to the sense of grandeur and something indescribable, maybe spiritual, that I don't truly understand. Similarly, a picnic in an orchard helps smooth out my anxious brow and connects me with living things that aren't human. Trees can't talk back, they can't trigger my anxiety – and, crucially, they don't remind me about Norma in Wyoming.

# 38. Meet my anxiety buddy Emily

159

As well as Derek, I have an anxiety buddy called Emily who is calm and encourages me to question my behaviour and my anxiety. She's Derek's worst enemy. Just imagine good and evil clashing.

My buddy Emily is a combination of my most level-headed friend Simon, the Dalai Lama, Spider-Man, a sloth called Truffle I met once at London Zoo, Winnie the Pooh and my late Great Aunt Audrey whose response to 97 per cent of problems was, 'Oh, bugger it all, why not have an éclair, sweetie?', which, you know, can help too.

When anxiety comes and Derek starts spouting his nonsense, I get Emily to materialise. She comes wearing orange thigh-length boots, a yellow trench coat, a fedora hat and effortlessly cool glasses. God knows why she dresses this way – my brain is so mystifying. She has this smile that says, 'Everything is going to be OK,' and a soothing, sensible disposition. Over the years I've tried so hard to physically turn into her, but sadly it's never worked. The current limitations of transgressive body morphing are a disgrace.

I use Emily to counteract Derek. They don't talk to each other – that would get a bit complicated when my mind is already playing tricks – but I initiate a conversation with her.

ME: I think Patrick is having an affair.

EMILY: What makes you think that?

ME: I found a long hair in the bathroom.

EMILY: Anything else?

ME: No.

EMILY: Did you ask him about the hair?

ME: He said he didn't know whose it was.

EMILY: Did you ask if he was having an affair?

ME: I'm afraid I did, and he said no.

EMILY: Right.

ME: Well, that's just what someone who *is* having an affair would say, isn't it?

EMILY: But it's also what someone *not* having an affair would say.

ME: He goes out for walks at lunchtime. I bet he sees them then.

EMILY: Who?

ME: Keep up! The person he's having an affair with. The person with the long hair. The chief suspect.

EMILY: How long does he go out for at lunchtime?

ME: He has a twenty-minute walk by the sea, so he says. Sometimes he does some shopping.

EMILY: So, you think this person lives near enough to walk to their house, spend time with them and still bring back a litre of light soya milk?

ME: And sometimes some yoghurt.

EMILY: And sometimes some yoghurt.

ME: Well, yes.

EMILY: Any other reason to suspect him?

ME: No.

EMILY: Has he had an affair before?

ME: Well, no. I mean, not that I know about. Would he tell me? I doubt it. We don't know, do we? I mean, maybe he has a different person in each port.

EMILY: Port? Does he work at sea?

ME: No.

EMILY: He's not an officer in the Merchant Navy?

ME: No.

EMILY: So, he doesn't go to sea at all and therefore doesn't spend his days off in international ports?

ME: No.

EMILY: And this long hair . . .

ME: Exhibit A.

EMILY: Don't be ridiculous.

ME: Sorry.

EMILY: This hair . . .

ME: Yes.

EMILY: It's not his hair?

ME: He has short hair.

EMILY: OK, has anyone been to visit recently who *has* long hair?

ME: No.

EMILY: Think again please.

ME: Maybe.

EMILY: Maybe?

ME: Possibly.

EMILY: Possibly?

ME: My sister, brother-in-law and three nieces came to visit last week.

EMILY: And do any of them have long hair?

ME: Yes.

EMILY: How many of them?

ME: I, ummm . . . I . . . don't want to say.

EMILY: Tell me.

ME: Four of them.

EMILY: Is it more likely that the long hair came from one of them?

ME: It may be a contributing factor in this particular case.

EMILY: It's not a 'case'.

ME: No.

EMILY: So, is that settled?

ME: Yes.

EMILY: Are you OK?

ME: Yes. Thank you.

Emily calms me down; she gets me thinking more logically. The aim is not to stop the anxiety altogether, because most anxiety we can't help feeling, but we can decide how we respond to it – and Emily helps me with that.

It works because there is a small part of us that knows the answers to the questions, and externalising it and bringing in an invented character helps visualisation.

Go forth and create your own anxiety buddy. Who knows what my imagination was doing when it created Emily, but it helps massively for me to have a clear picture of her. Try drawing your anxiety buddy if that helps, and maybe keep a picture of them on your phone, in your purse or wallet or in your thigh-length boots.

The only real requirement is that your buddy can talk, which is why I think it's better to have a human rather than, say, a sheep, because we're more familiar with how humans talk. If it were a sheep it would all be 'baa, baa, baa' (which just sounds a bit woolly).

# 39. Use your sense(s)

A goldfish bowl has been placed over my head.

I can see blurry figures, hear distorted sounds and sense an odd, lingering, putrid smell. No one can reach me. Life is playing out in a blur; it is a film that has malfunctioned, a distorted nightmare that is terrifying, yet I'm utterly disconnected from it. I can feel pain, hopelessness and terror; they're swimming inside the bowl and seeping into my head.

It's not the nicest of feelings. I'd much rather be sat in a summer meadow playing with an exuberant puppy.

When anxiety hits, our world changes, our perspective alters and it's like being in a dream. Our usual reality is distorted to the extent that we can't connect with the world outside in a 'normal' way. Everything goes quiet; we can't smell, taste or even see properly.

We need to take off the goldfish bowl and reconnect with the world. Reconnecting means consciously feeling all our senses and acknowledging who we are and where we are. This helps combat anxiety.

Think of it like a fantasy computer game. The Dark Master of Anxiety has stunned you, and you feel hopeless. You feel around for weapons but there's nothing in reach. However, on a previous quest you earned the reward of heightening all your senses (you can tell I don't design many computer games), so this is what you do. You listen as hard as you can for what you can **hear**, in this case the breath of the Dark Master and the faint roar of a melancholy dragon.

Then you **smell** deeply and notice the Dark Master's garlicky breath, the burnt remains of a peasant village and the dung of a passing unicorn. Then you **feel** around for what you can touch: a prickly bush nearby, and the stony path leading from the bewitched castle. Then you look closely and you can **see** the sun setting over the enchanted mountain and rain falling on the magical meadow.

I hope you get my point. Fear not, I'm not about to create any computer games any time soon, or write fantasy novels for that matter.

My anxiety often happens on the way to work while I'm waiting for my train. I listen to the footsteps on the platform, the pigeons flapping their wings on the roof or the cough of someone nearby. Then I look at the weeds on the railway track, the faded yellow line near the platform edge and the crack in the wall opposite. Then I smell someone's takeaway coffee, the disinfectant from the toilets or a whiff of perfume from someone who has just walked by.

It is not a tick-box exercise, so don't worry if you can't smell any unicorn dung. It's just a way of removing the goldfish bowl and bringing reality slowly back into view when anxiety has taken it away.

167

# 40. Make a plan, Mary-Anne

I monitor my anxiety, and keep records.

I track what triggers it and what makes it worse.
I rate it somewhere between 1 and 10, depending
on how awful it is. I also record what I do to manage my
anxiety and how much the action I take helps to reduce
it. On the surface this might seem overly analytical and
geeky, and in truth it is both those things, but it's also
useful.

I know it's a pain in the arse having to write all this
stuff down, but anxiety alters your reality and your perspective; and, if your memory is anything like mine, unless
you write it down it can be hard to recall how you felt. My
plan is just recorded on my phone, so it's not complicated,
and certainly isn't anything any well-respected cognitive
behavioural psychologist would enter as an abstract for an
international conference in Gdansk, but it helps me. Here's
an example:

| | |
|---|---|
| Trigger: | Worried that I'm not going to sleep tonight. |
| Score out of 10: | 3. |
| Action: | Go for a cycle. Read my book. |
| Result: | Felt better for going outside. Reading before bed helped distract me. |

You can refer back to this whenever you need to. Find out what triggered your anxiety, see what you did and whether it helped, then take the same action, or try something different if that one didn't work. It is helpful to see evidence that taking action to work on your anxiety does produce results. By taking a positive action you're not just at the mercy of anxiety, trying to dodge the cannon balls it hurls at you from the sky. Experiment, change things if necessary and do whatever helps – as long as you're not hurting people or animals.

I've discovered fantastic techniques and skills to help me since I started writing down my anxiety plan. For example, some time ago my anxiety was incredibly high before going on holiday, because I was terrified that I would inadvertently leave the cooker on and that would kill the cat and burn down the flat. ('Kill the cat and burn down the flat' is also the name of my new single coming out next year.) So, what I did was photograph the cooker knobs to remind myself when I was away that I had turned them off. I trust the photographic evidence on my phone more than I trust myself.

I'm quite sure that 'those in the know', like a Gdansk-bound psychologist, would not recommend this. Instead, they would tell me to trust myself and accept that worrying is part of life. But sod that. It works brilliantly for me. Now when I'm at the airport about to go on holiday, I look at the pictures of the cooker knobs – and the bathroom taps too, I must admit – and it makes me feel so much better. It means I have a great holiday and don't worry about fire or flood. If I were to do this every time I left the house, that would be a concern, but it's only when I go away and the flat is empty, so in my mind this is a complete win.

You see there is controllable and uncontrollable anxiety, and the cooker knobs scenario is an example of controllable anxiety. Uncontrollable anxiety is when you hear a report that North Korea has acquired a nuclear weapon so huge it can wipe out Saturn. There's not a lot you can do about that unless you have the Supreme Leader's e-mail address – and I'm suspecting you don't, so why trouble yourself? It doesn't stop you worrying; it's just that controllable anxiety is well suited to written plans.

When it comes to uncontrollable anxiety, I have a few basic questions that Emily my anxiety buddy (see Chapter 38) asks me.

- Do you need to worry about this?
- Is it appropriate to be anxious about this?
- Can anyone help you?
- Is there something you can do to help yourself?

171

You can then use the tips in this book to help you out. Marvellous, eh?

Up yours, anxiety!

# Acknowledgements

Thank you to Tom Asker at Little, Brown.
As always, thank you to Patrick.

JAMES WITHEY

How to Tell
**Depression**

TO

# PISS
# OFF

## 40 Ways to Get
## Your Life Back

# How To Tell Depression to Piss Off

*Available now*

## Depression sucks, but you don't.

Trying to manage the range of symptoms that depression throws at you is like navigating the dark ocean floor when you are without a torch and don't know how to swim. How do you manage something that feels utterly unmanageable? How do you get through each day when depression is telling you you're a worthless lump of camel spleen? What you need is a guide. A really good one. You need to know what works and what to do.

This book gives you 40 ways to get to a better place with depression. They are born out of the author's personal experience of clinical depression and his many years of working as a counsellor helping people with their mental health. James lives with depression and knows its lies, the traps it makes and how to dodge when it starts spitting bile in your face. Nice, eh?

At whatever point you're at with your depression, this book can help and provide some laughs along the way – hooray! – because you really need it with this bloody illness.